Morgellons Among Us

Morgellons Among Us

Bobbi Devine

Copyright © 2014 by Bobbi Devine.

ISBN:	Softcover	978-1-4990-4048-7
	eBook	978-1-4990-4049-4

All rights reserved. No part of this book may be reproduced or transmitted in any form or by any means, electronic or mechanical, including photocopying, recording, or by any information storage and retrieval system, without permission in writing from the copyright owner.

Any people depicted in stock imagery provided by Thinkstock are models, and such images are being used for illustrative purposes only.
Certain stock imagery © Thinkstock.

This book was printed in the United States of America.

Rev. date: 08/18/2014

To order additional copies of this book, contact:
Xlibris LLC
1-888-795-4274
www.Xlibris.com
Orders@Xlibris.com

CONTENTS

Dedication 7

Introduction 11

Chapter One 13

Chapter Two 19

Chapter Three 28

Chapter Four 31

Chapter Five 36

Chapter Six 39

Chapter Seven 42

Chapter Eight 47

Chapter Nine 71

Chapter Ten 77

Chapter Eleven 80

Chapter Twelve 82

New Chapter: New Me 82

Dedication

To my friend and confidante Alan D. Johnson. Your research is effortless, your knowledge, endless. Al, you've been critical to my healing.

To Clifford Carnicom, your tireless research to get to the root of this problem has placed me where I am today. Without your sacrifice and commitment we wouldn't be going forward.

To my beautiful daughters Jaclynn and Brooke, Greg, son-in-law Ryan, grandchildren Everah and Vienna, we fought long and hard to overcome this adversity. We won! My heartfelt love and thanks to all of you. I give my God, Jesus Christ, all the glory.

Sincerely,

Bobbi Devine

About a decade ago I heard a program on shortwave radio, possibly "The Power Hour", with guest Clifford Carnicom. The program described an unusual condition, being called Morgellons' disease, affecting a number of people who reported having colored fibers coming out of their skin. Their physicians were not helpful, often referring the patients to psychiatrists for treatment of "delusions of parasitosis".

Several months later Bobbi Devine told me she had "wires and colored fibers coming out of her skin". I told her about the independent research of Carnicom, who has tediously analyzed the infra-red spectra of these fibers in an attempt to identify their chemical structure.

I suspect Morgellons' is a bio-warfare agent, although agencies like the Center for Disease Control (CDC), and the American Medical Association (AMA), appear to be engaging in cover-up and propaganda in this matter.

Alan D. Johnson
Hibbing, Minnesota
14 January 2014

Introduction

How often have you experienced a physical reaction or change that shocked you beyond your understanding? I'm talking about a single event so absurd and unheard of that you were afraid to tell anyone about it. This book is a personal journey of my own experience with Morgellons disease—a disease that has been kept hush-hush for years by they that know about it. It has been said that it is caused by a chemical knowingly (or unknowingly?) released by the government. It has been leaked into our society in which it is banned and found to be a genetically modified product poisoning many innocent people. It is a disease difficult to fully describe, because not one of its harrowing symptoms can be compared to that of any other disease. Some symptoms are so traumatizing that many of the disease's victims commit suicide. Others suffer in silence. I did just that. After ten long, arduous years of solitude, I have recovered, and I have chosen to share my testimony with you. In this profound and self-revealing book, I hope to help other victims and their families to cope with all the life-changing events that can take place. For all the people suffering from this wretched condition, I hope this brings you comfort, knowing that you are not alone. For families suffering with an afflicted loved one, I hope this gives you peace and some guidance through it all.

I won't stop fighting until Morgellons is a household word. I won't stop fighting until people are informed. I won't stop fighting until people see our needs.

Chapter One

Blisters? I've never broken out in blisters. Only when I was sunburned or wore shoes that didn't fit correctly. This breakout was unusual. I remember standing at the basement stairs, carrying laundry. I suddenly felt a stinging, crawling sensation. I pulled my sleeves up and watched as one blister after another popped out of my skin with no warning. They started on my left wrist and uniformly produced a pattern in a zigzag fashion up my arm and over my shoulder. I bet if I would have measured them, they would have been almost identical in size and distance apart from one another. Once the blisters had finished spreading on the left arm, the right arm began breaking out in the exact same manner. I knew this wasn't a typical situation. I had a gut feeling that I was in for a challenge. In all my forty-three years, I had never seen or heard of anything like this. It felt and appeared as though they had a mind of their own. These frightening things gripped my heart with fear. They struck a chord within me that I never knew I had.

I had so many questions, so many fears. I decided that it was a mind-set that I had to snap out of. Yes, I had to convince myself that I was overreacting, panicking. It was time to ignore this and get on with my daily tasks. Yet I couldn't snap out of it. Deep in my heart I knew that a battle had just begun. I was sure that life as I knew it was changing. But for how long? I had been working in health care and had been raising my two daughters as a single parent. I purchased a home and lived there for two years before I began having these problems. As I now understand, it takes eighteen months to get full-blown Morgellons after being initially exposed. It is apparent that my physical issues were wreaking havoc on me. I suffered serious pain that the doctors were calling polymyalgia. I couldn't think straight and had difficulty concentrating. Within months, I was fired from two jobs and realized I would be fired from a third, most likely. It was time to stop working and get into disability assistance with the intent of taking care of myself with all the strength that I had. At this time, I sold my home and moved into a low-income housing complex—my only hope of making it. After moving in and getting settled, which took about four months, I had my initial blister outbreak.

I started to recognize other odd things happening. One night, I went to shut the light on my nightstand. As I reached and extended my arm, I saw a very fine layer of what appeared to be blue cotton candy. I was so stressed out. Whom can I talk to? Who will hear me? Afraid, I kept it to myself. This "blue cotton candy" was evenly distributed around my arm. Baffled, I wiped my arms off as I watched it roll up into balls of lint and cotton ball-sized fiber. I saved this stuff and placed it in a jar. When I left it in the jar, the fiber turned white, gray, and black. When I later took it out of the jar and held it, the fiber became white, light blue, and a vibrant, darker blue. This happened once I touched it. Oh, the mental stress this had on me. Really, who would believe me? In true embarrassment, I tucked it all away and didn't say a word. The pain within had begun. I had stress, nausea, headaches . . . I was alone. There was no support group for people like me. I truly felt scared, alienated, confused. I was seriously frightened.

It was only a couple of nights after the cotton candy incident that I had another physical sign of this disease. As I was changing into my nightshirt, I noticed shiny gold particles all over my chest. I looked like a porcupine! There was nothing funny about it. As I looked closer, they looked similar to tinsel, glitter, gold metallic slivers, and shards of gold metal. They were really sharp and painful. I tried to pluck each one out, and I bled and cried through it. I had no one to comfort me or hold me. I lay there fighting a panic attack as I kept telling myself to slow down, relax. It will get better. "Really?" I asked myself. "Really?"

I gathered up all the slivers and such and tucked them away in a jar. I started to wash up with organic products, not really knowing what to use. I had no doctor. These are the frightening thoughts one goes through as they struggle with Morgellons. About five days later, I had to go to the emergency room. My chest was hot, red, and full of infected lesions. It was insane. The doctor came in and asked how he could help me. I was losing my ability to communicate well. Weakened by my condition, I just held back the anger and tears as I opened my shirt. He cringed. He was just as confused as I was. I told him about the slivers. He had nothing to say about them. I left there with a few bandages and some antibiotics, but no diagnosis.

I started going from doctor to doctor as more symptoms appeared. I began naming the things that came out of me. My next nightmare I call "guitar picks," which were small cream-colored plastic things. I called them this because they were similar to them and were just as hard. They would push with force underneath my skin, trying to break through. It was painful and unsightly, so I began breaking my skin on top of the protrusion so it would find its way out. Usually, I would take tweezers and get it out myself.

I no longer could rest. I had no comfort whatsoever. No one could comfort me, not knowing what I was going through. I still hadn't told anyone what was really going on; I just mentioned the obvious—painful lesions that were not healing. I became a recluse. It became harder and harder to think. I had to find a doctor and a diagnosis *now*. I was afraid that my mental and emotional problems from this disorder were going to deem me housebound or bedridden for the most part and unable to get any help alone. With help I went from doctor to doctor, clinic to clinic. I was getting nowhere. Not one of them could give me a confident diagnosis. It was a guessing game. After about eighteen to twenty-four months, I was told that I needed to see a psychotherapist. Oh no, I was not going to let anyone tell me that I was delusional. If I hadn't saved the specimens in small ziplock baggies, I would have believed that I needed that therapy. I held strong to what I saw and to what I was going through. This is the first time that I realized that going to a doctor was no longer going to be the source of comfort that it had been for most of my life. The doctors acted like they didn't know any more than anyone else had, and I had no reason to believe otherwise; I may as well have gone to a cashier at a fast food restaurant. Reality struck me. I had to teach my doctors about what I'm going through. Now was the time to find one that would listen to me. I was determined to do this. The hunt was on.

I had setbacks as I became sicker and sicker. I wasn't able to get out of bed too often. One year, I remember going to bed in April and waking up in September. I couldn't recall a thing between those months. I generally had times that I was awake; however, I wasn't conscientious, and I was in horrible pain. At this point, seeing a doctor wasn't easy. The effort was tremendously strenuous, physically and mentally. Although I was awake, I was hardly aware of my surroundings. I knew I would die in that bed if I didn't get up. Nothing concerned me anymore but survival alone. My hair, makeup clothes, weight—they didn't matter. I went to the doctor in my pajamas! I was in need of pain relief. I knew the risks I was taking, but I no longer had options. Again, seeking comfort from a doctor was impossible. I lay in bed, grabbing my quilt, white-knuckled, and crying day after day and month after month, until the thought came to me to write to the doctors. I did just that. "Sending six letters out should get me the help I need," I thought. Well, it did. I received a few refusals, but one doctor said he would help me if I went into his office. With the help of a friend, I made it to the appointment. He prescribed me OxyContin. It was such a blessing at the time! Imagine being all tensed up, and you can't relax for months, and then all of a sudden you get a medication that loosens all that tension. I literally went limp for the first few doses from the brutal exhaustion. I hoped that having pain-free moments would give me the ability to do a little bit each day. "Thank you, Jesus", I thought. I knew it would help.

 I couldn't cry out for help any louder. Occasionally, they would hospitalize me. I was hooked up to an antibiotic drip and given fluids and something, too, for pain. Dehydration was a huge problem for me. I was convinced that all the fibers in me absorbed any fluid, and I was always dehydrated and weakened because of it. The dehydration caused seizures. I wrestled with various infections, some large, some small. Several of these infections had to be lanced and drained, and some of the lesions never healed as I was sure they were carrying loads of bacteria. The lesions changed often, spreading to other areas of my skin and changing shape, size, color, and texture. They were powerfully controlling me and my body. I was infiltrated with substances that I couldn't explain. I felt it necessary to start inspecting these particles closer, with hope of getting a better idea of what was going on. I was aiming at using all the strength that I had to attempt to find something, to find anything that might help ease any discomfort or slow down this vicious cycle.

As I started to watch the lesions, I began to learn a lot. I watched fibers come out of my skin. They were cotton like, often metallic and in a variety of colors such as red, white, black, green, yellow, orange, blue, pink, and even purple. The majority of them, however, were gray, white, and blue. When I was awake, I would study these particles. It took its toll on me. I had to get out of those four walls that I had been staring at for well over a year. On occasion, I'd stop by and see a friend of mine, Alan. Al is a chemist and a genius. He got my mind off myself for a while. I even think that I may have slept there a few nights. I was probably sitting up for all I knew! Al is legally blind and getting worse, so it was hard to know what he was aware of, if anything besides my voice. Nonetheless, he is brilliant, and I enjoy listening to him and all that he researches. Al dots all his i's and crosses all his t's. He is always learning. He is always reading or listening to shortwave radio. He is always seeking what is going on in the world. Al never misses a beat.

During one visit, he was talking and said, "Bobbie, you'll never believe this one! I've been listening to *The Power Hour* on the radio." He said that there is a rare disorder starting to surface where people are pulling fibers out of their skin! My jaw dropped, and it felt as if my eyes popped out of my head. I yelled, "Al! I have that! I've never told anyone, Al! I didn't think they would believe me!" He then proceeded to tell me the little that was known about it. For the first time in years, I had found out what was wrong with me—Morgellons disease. *Stenotrophomonas maltophilia.*

Chapter Two

I know now that it certainly was not in my head. Incidentally, I never believed that it was. I was always confident of that fact. I then went online to CarnicomInstitute.org. Cliff Carnicom has a thorough test online to see if you possibly have Morgellons disease. Unfortunately, I passed with flying colors. I cannot recall the website; however, I was the eight hundredth recorded case in the United States. "Now that I am certain of my condition, what do I do?", I thought. Much to my surprise, the doctors still didn't believe me and called it everything from dermatitis to something as plain and simple as picking. I soon found a wonderful nurse practitioner in Northern Minnesota. She alone helped me more than a dozen doctors had. She contacted the finest facility out there, and they told her this: "The sooner your patient realizes she's her own best doctor, the better off she'll be." My heart sank. I now felt even more alone. Yet I still had my faith in God. I sought him daily, and he had to have given me strength. I had neither hope nor reason to go on. God gave me hope. I wanted to die everyday, yet something whispered deep in my heart and soul that said, "I will be healed." Morgellons disease, Ernst disease, *Stenotrophomonas multifilia*, whatever they call it, I'm ready to educate myself and start fighting this battle!

Information on this condition wasn't easy to find. With all that was in me and in my friend Al, we had found pertinent information. We found many articles. One of them said that a Morgellons patient should not ingest or use anything with copper, iron, hydrogen peroxide, or bleach just to name a few. I personally take these things seriously, depending on the trust that I have in the writers of the articles, of course. I, myself, have experienced that we are all different. I read to not use petroleum jelly, yet VapoRub worked wonders for me, and I used it often. It softened my skin and slowed down activity in my lesions. My personal advice is that everyone needs to experiment with different creams, lotions, oils, etc. Organic and hypoallergenic are the best choice.

Find a doctor that will research Morgellons for you. I found Cliff Carnicom's advice to be right on (carnicominstitute.org). I followed it the best I could. The things that I did may or may not necessarily help you, but I encourage you to try them! Find the remedies that work for you. It's trial and error.

I want to share with you several of the symptoms I suffered with. Brain fog (this is a big one) was devastating and debilitating. Brain fog! What an understatement! I could only live in the here and now. I had to forget planning as I honestly could not think fifteen minutes in advance. A girlfriend watched out for me one day when I wanted to cook something. She had to call me every ten to fifteen minutes to check on me and make sure that I hadn't forgotten something on the stove. She had to walk me through things one step at a time. I couldn't follow directions; they were overwhelming. If it wasn't for her, I wouldn't have been able to do the little that I had done. We lived about eight to ten blocks apart, and she always tried to get me to go for a walk or to go over for coffee. I recall going there, yet I wasn't alert enough to remember what was talked about, etc. I was afraid to go out. Brain fog made me feel as though I had the mentality of a child; I was aware of very little surrounding me. I had many blackouts. They would last for hours or what felt like months. I recall one morning that I was making coffee. I poured myself a cup and sat on the edge of the couch. As I watched television, I went to take a sip of my coffee, and it was cold. I was convinced my new coffee maker was defective. I went into the kitchen to see what the problem was, only to notice that it was 5:00 PM! I made the coffee at 9:00 AM and sat on the couch for eight hours without moving! It felt like ten minutes. This was very troubling to me. My concept of time was so screwed up that I couldn't imagine all the awful things that could go wrong because of it. Brain fog is such a serious symptom of Morgellons Disease! It is so scary. I lost my ability to reason, my concept of time, and my ability to concentrate . . . it was gone. I would try to fight the fog with little results. I was always afraid of looking confused as I was. I was in no shape to socialize, yet I knew getting out could only be good for me.

My girlfriend Mary was such a god send. I needed to get out of the house so desperately. I wondered where I could go and what I could do. My first thought was to see Mary. I hadn't seen her in 30 years! I don't know why I didn't think of someone closer to me. I think it was the short term/long term affects that this disease has on your memory. I couldn't remember things that just happened but at times remembered bits and pieces of the past. Mary would drive and we would go digging for old bottles. It was a blast and temporarily got me out of my misery. We found all kinds of strange things that kept us busy. I was still very sick. I still suffered . . . but it was a relief not to focus on it for awhile. I mention several times that I didn't have any help and I never was able to get help at home. But friends like these are such a blessing. They got me out of the house. This is priceless.

I had another friend that would bring me for short rides, often in scrubs or pajamas. I was that lost and out of touch. It was so difficult going to my children's school functions (PTA, concerts, plays). Their father picked me up. I had to wear dress clothes, of course. This took all day to prepare for. I was way too sick to do anything that called for proper social protocol. I couldn't escape judgment of other parents. I was so weak and shaky. I had no balance and would almost fall down often. How embarrassing. I often felt bullied; bullying is not just a problem in K-12. Adults will pick on other adults just as much. I found it rude. The looks, the comments—it was humiliating. People I once respected turned on me. It hurt. Of course, I grieved and prayed for this crazy world. I applauded George Bush Sr. when he said, "We need a kinder and gentler nation." That was evident in my situation.

Brain fog caused many other problems. One could experience tics, slurred/stuttered speech, memory loss, amnesia, and being very desensitized about one's surroundings. The amnesia was such that I forgot parts of my life. I didn't forget it all, but I couldn't picture many scenarios. I'd look at pictures of my past and be totally out of touch with them. I knew the person in the picture was me, yet I couldn't recall a thing. Some of that returned during my recovery, and some are still coming back to me. It's a lengthy road to healing, that's for sure. Tourette's syndrome was also on the list of Morgellons symptoms, and I did suffer, too, with that, off and on. No, I didn't yearn to yell out profanities. When I felt the urge to scream, I would hum very loudly. I remember humming one night for over eight hours. It was frightening. Don't let it drive you crazy as "this too shall pass." Stay headstrong. You have to have faith in God and remain headstrong to survive this. So many of the zany symptoms of Morgellons can make you feel like you're losing your mind. Stay strong! Don't fall apart when doctor after doctor tells you that it's all in your head. Remember, you have valuable knowledge that few people know about. You are so important to many! Keep fighting! Hold on to that knowledge, for one day, when you are stronger (or even healed), many people will need to hear you speak about your experience. There will be so many people crying out for help, for comfort. Will you be there for them? Can you? Please fight to be there. Can you see how important you are to so many people? You, my friend, will be the answer to many prayers out there. Just hold on! "With God, all things are possible."

It's so easy to bury your head under that shame and never want to come out. When you can come out, start small. Bathe daily. It sounds so small and so easy, but it's huge. Change your linens and put clean pajamas on. That in itself felt like a full-time job. When I read about reinfection, I realized that you have to stay clean. Never wear your clothes twice. Don't sleep on the same sheets twice in a row if you can avoid it. When I was too weak I would use a linen lint remover; they came in a sticky tape or a shaver type instrument. These are of great help in times of tremendous need. Always bathe in one-fourth cup baking soda water or one-half cup apple cider vinegar water. I put it in the water while the tub is filling up. Bathing like this helps keep the lesions calm and the pH in your body closer to neutral. If your lesions aren't really busy, use oatmeal in your water. It's excellent at helping your skin retain moisture.

This is so much work for someone as sick as Morgellons people get. It makes me want to cry just thinking about it. I had very little help. I'm sure I wasn't able to keep up with these things; I fought and did my best. If you have a caretaker make sure that your laundry is done and your floors are always clean. The particles are all over! They not only collect as dust does, they multiply! Yes, the Morgellons debris will enlarge and multiply. Small pieces of it will fall off of a large piece and leave a whole new piece of Morgellons to thrive! They are absolute monsters! I read somewhere that Morgellons was still alive after enduring temperatures well over 1,000 degrees! They thrive anywhere. I know that you will find a lot of it where ever there is static electricity. You'll find them stuck on blankets, in your hair, on TV screens etc. You'll need to find the necessary help for vacuuming and dusting. It is so, so important.

When I was at my worst stage of this condition I was basically bedridden. I believe that I lost consciousness often. I didn't know what was happening and I still don't know what all happened. All I know is that my mind shut off and I laid there. I could communicate often, yet their were times that I couldn't open my eyes or my mouth. I could hear everything around me but I couldn't move! This is something that no one should have to go thru alone. I think everyone thought that I was sleeping all of the time! I slept a lot but was awake a lot more often than anyone knew. I wished someone was sitting by me holding my hand, singing to me, rubbing my feet . . . anything! I longed to have someone sitting at my side. If you are reading this and have a loved one with this disease, please comfort them in any way possible. So many Morgellons patients are being blamed for their.condition, and they are ignored. No! These people are suffering to the fullest extent and need support and comfort. As you know, I made it thru this with little help. There were times I felt as though I would fail to thrive. I was sure I was going to lay there and die. I didn't see a reason to wake up in my condition, I'd be no help to anyone. I had no consistent encouragement and my loved ones didn't know how badly I needed it. So for those of you suffering alone as I did, I want you to know that I'm doing this because I care. I really do care. I beg to family and friends, please don't overlook their needs. God will bless you for all your work and effort. Keep strong. It's not a small task but stay strong for each other. Morgellons is so all consuming.

Have you ever been in the process of falling asleep and right before you do you have a rapid twitch that instantly wakes you? That's exactly what the tics feel like. Tics were a constant and annoying symptom from the brain fog (I believe). Any part of your body will twitch unpredictably. My head, neck, eyes, eyelids, mouth, arms and legs all had these spasms. It's embarrassing and out of our control. They happen at any given time day and night. My family and friends would see this when they were around. I'm still not sure if they thought I was kidding or being dramatic. Maybe they understood. I still haven't talked to them about everything! They haven't asked. My family could very well have been just as afraid and confused as I was. They probably didn't know what to do or say. Be bold and communicate with one another! It would be nice if you could find answers, at least to know where the patient is coming from and what their immediate needs are. Any needs met, however small, will give them strength and reduce the dread in their day. Trust me, they need you! It will give them a reason to hang on and fight.

Slow? Slurring? Unstable on your feet? Yes, all of these come with Morgellons. My disorganized thinking made me feel dizzy at times! I was a mess. When I was unsteady on my feet I had the sense to use a cane. It helped. When it became really bad I used a walker. I recall going to a church function and feeling as though I was going to faint. I leaned to one side, unaware that it was a cardboard wall. It didn't fall but I did get bad looks from people for leaning up against it. "Wow",

I thought. They must think I'm a real idiot for leaning up against a fake wall! I felt so humiliated, so embarrassed. Being unaware of my surroundings was a huge problem for me. I simply was not alert. I wasn't concientous.

Talking was so difficult. I simply couldn't organize my thoughts, neither did I have enough strength to talk. Many times I knew what I wanted to say but to no avail. I acted very slow or even handicap as I was at the time. Their were times that my thinking was at its best and I was still unable to actually follow thru with any plans I tried to make. I called it mental stuttering. My thoughts were all over the place. I verbally stuttered as well. It took a long time to get a point across and to register what someone else was saying. I no longer could have two simultaneous thoughts. I couldn't keep up with a normal conversation either. Staying home, on one hand, was far more peaceful than trying to fit into a crowd that I know longer could relate to. Even though I hated being home alone, it became way to much work trying to keep up with all the activity going on around me. It's fair to say that I was over-whelmed with anything around me . . . it was too much.

Laying in bed day after day, month after month and year after year was obviously draining to me. I worried about my family all of the time. Where were they? Were they okay? Were their needs being met? I knew they were out and about living their lives. I missed them so much. What I really missed was being healthy and able to be with them. Even though they lived with me I seldom saw them. They had all of their school and church activities (thank God!) . . . and I slept most of the time. It broke my heart. I literally cried every day. Sometimes I cried all day. My children were growing up without me! How could this be? All I ever asked for is a close, loving family. I never asked for much, yet what I wanted and needed was being taken from me. My pain was deep. I felt a pain like I had been stabbed in the chest. What about their pain? They didn't ask for this either! "Oh God" I prayed, don't let this carry on. I need to see them grow up. They need me here. What about when they marry and have children of their own? Will I STILL be in bed? What's worse? Should I lie here waiting? Or would it be mercy to bail out? Hmm . . . a decision had to be made. I can't go on feeling like this. I can't continue to lie here crying. It's time for a serious change. I'm desperate for answers. "God give me strength to live or take me. Don't let me destroy my family like this God. Should I leave? God forbid that this last memory of me be such an ugly, heartbreaking one! Let's get it over with. I can't watch this show any longer", I thought.

Chapter Three

I have no choice but to familiarize myself with my condition. No one else is going to do it. I knew I had to take a closer look at what was going on. It was time, today, now. It doesn't matter if I feel good or not. I'm awake and that's precious time. I couldn't wait any longer to educate myself and to spare myself any more misery . . . if it was possible.

One of the first lesions I studied was brown and felt like sandpaper. When I looked at it magnified it resembled a group of burrs that stick to your pant legs as you walk into the woods. As I watched these burrs they were slowly swelling. I continued watching for quite some time. It looked perfectly round, rough and sandy. As it slowly swelled it appeared to be cupped by a variety of pieces of similar debris, possibly broken pieces of the burr itself. As I watched it for hours four silver tubes started to unfold underneath the burr as they were holding it in place. I couldn't believe what I was seeing and only wished that I could somehow record what I was seeing. I wished someone else was there to witness it all. I wasn't able to get a photo of it unfortunately. Visualize this; four pieces of metal looking tubes pushing the burr right off of my skin! When it did this several of them did it at the same time. I studied my skin and in the process the burrs were bursting and becoming their own group of smaller burrs.

They felt like sand. When they popped, they scattered down the inside of my arm, many of them clinging to my skin as they slid down. At that point the process started again. It all happened so fast. After so many hours of studying, this made it all worth it. However, recognizing the process of reinfection was terrible. Once they pop and spread you have a larger lesion with all the fibers, burrs etc. coming out of them . . . which cause you complete and utter discomfort. As I studied these I never took one speck for granted. I tried to look at each and every one of them (of course I knew I really wasn't, their were far too many!). The thought of throwing one away that was profoundly different and full of new and interesting developments disturbed me.

The burrs were so scary. When they broke out I couldn't stop them. I would take tweezers, needles, fingernail clippers, and anything else I could find to remove them, but they were their for good. The only way of getting them off was to have a doctor do a biopsy. That in itself wasn't the answer either. They would just grow back. I just wanted them to go away forever. In my sick and desperate state of mind I was losing my patience. I started to remove these things by myself with whatever instrument I could find . . . even a box cutter. I certainly wasn't in my right mind. I was so exhausted from it all. I wanted it to be over. I couldn't take it any more.

A new and vicious particle began bearing its' ugly self with full force. I call it 'ammo' as in ammunition. I could see one here and there but not enough of them to feel too threatened . . . so I thought. It starts as a fluid oozing out of one of my pores, onto my skin. That fluid then weaves into my skin, back up and down again . . . repeatedly in a straight line. It literally looked like someone had sewn a top stitch on my arm with a sewing machine. Each and every weave up and down were identical in size and shape. To make things even more interesting, I could grab the end of the fluid when it dried and pull on it. It would come out of my skin exactly like a piece of thread! As these 'threads' multiplied and weaved patterns into my skin I became overwhelmed. Now what? I was so tired of the constant activity. I started to yank the 'threads' out of me. I couldn't keep up with them. I had pinched and pulled about a dozen of them off. I went to throw them away and they had started to meld with my skin! How awful. They were reabsorbing into my finger tips! This is how easy it is to reinfect yourself with this stuff . . . ugh! I don't believe that Morgellons' is THAT catchy. However, with symptoms like these I'd say it would be wise to treat it as though it's highly contagious!

Chapter Four

To prevent this stuff from spreading I did a lot of different things, mostly trial and error. A lot of this came from Cliff Carnicom and some of his suggestions. I bathed and showered constantly. I never felt clean, yet I knew it was necessary to attempt to be. I also used a lot of oregano oil, an excellent oil to prevent bacteria and fungus. Peppermint oil was excellent too. It would cause the lesions to close for a while. This was good if you felt well enough to go out, (It prevents the particles from coming out of you for a little while). VapoRub was my favorite—I could breathe, my skin could breathe . . . I felt the best that I could considering the situation. When I felt well enough to go the store (rare!), I would say, "What perfume should I wear? Oregano? Peppermint? VapoRub?" Ha! I needed a sense of humor in times like that.

Another way of preventing the spreading is by covering yourself with tight clothing. Leggings are great. Tight, long-sleeved T-shirts slowed down the lesions' activity. The lesions need oxygen, so I suggest to not let them have much, or they will drive you crazy! But it's a lot of work. There are so many lotions etc. out there. Listen to advice on *The Power Hour*, CarnicomInstitute.org, Rense.com, and others that you can research. After much practice, you'll find the products that work for you.

As I got a closer look at each lesion and saw their ability to spread and cause long-term misery, I also named them "weapons" (as you probably know by now). They were just as scary and intimidating as a lethal weapon and I felt threatened by them.

Once you get some control over a Morgellons weapon, another one will pop up. This strange activity that I had observed sparked a growing interest in this ungodly condition.

I've known very little about this disease. I had read a variety of articles written by professionals at that time. A lot of things could only be assumed/guessed back then. Much research needed to be done on every detail of this uncommon disease. Many of the articles were written by believers of Morgellons, unbelievers, and people that thought it was a self-inflicted problem! Ugh! How awful to think someone would cut their skin open and plant balls of lint into it just to confuse doctors or get attention! That is crazy. I don't understand that thought process and believe people do go to great lengths for attention; this book and subject matter is not about that kind of story. People are not delusional, and it is not fabricated. I believe in a combination of statements by the best researchers out there. It's a poisoning by a product that is banned in the United States of America, a pesticide. Now that I know a few things about Morgellons disease, I keep my eyes open and my antennae up. I couldn't wait to learn more about this mystery disease!

My research and information came from late 2003 on. Of course, it was the best I could do with what I had. I didn't have much. My computer worked off and on. Hence, I lost quite a bit of my information. I wasn't able to function for lengths of time. When I was able to function, it certainly didn't mean that I could write, read, or dictate. It was awfully hard depending on myself for so much but I was determined.

Thus, it took ten years. Over the years, authors of the many articles I read would change or add to their work due to more discovered information and more findings. One had to be sharp to stay atop of it all. I could grasp a lot of it because I was experiencing it all. My goal was to gather as much knowledge as possible to make all Morgellons patients able to go forward, hoping all I had worked for would help them gain the strength to move ahead and desire to live. I wanted to influence as many people as possible and give them a hunger to know more, hoping that they would gain the strength and willpower to pass this torch to others along the way. I wanted someone to have the answers to "What is this?" and "Why? Who did this and for what reason?"

Without a doubt, I have forgotten a lot of previously remembered bits and pieces of the many facts being revealed over the years. However, in my frame of mind, that would be inevitable. The word had to get out about it, and I needed to start something. Now, I can hope that others will do the same and a pattern will erupt.

Over the years I went into Morgellons chat rooms online and witnessed a lot of panic. People were so afraid. People were on the verge of suicide. A few people commit suicide. No books were written at the time. People were desperate for more information on this subject. Things really weren't happening yet. Morgellons information needed to get on its' feet so to speak. I often wondered if I would see the day that this battle would begin. Now I ask, "Will I be there to watch us win it?". We will win it. I'm confident of it.

No one knows exactly where we are coming in contact with this; however, there is much speculation. It has been said, as I stated earlier, that the government has been accused of accidentally leaking this substance into our communities. It has been found in many water sources. It is a known fact from CarnicomInstitute.org that most Morgellons cases are in and around major airports. It has been found in airline fuel. Was it international terrorism and/or domestic terrorism? There doesn't seem to be any solid answer at the time of writing this.

When I realized what I had and how serious it was, I became very bitter. I thought that I knew what anger was. I was sure that I knew what it was like to be frightened and lonely. But I didn't. Morgellons is a tremendously heavy cross to bear. Every symptom is unbearable and uncontrollable. It's hard, but we need to fight so our cross doesn't become heavier with anger, hate, rage, jealousy, etc. I know it sounds crazy, but I encourage everyone affected with this to try to lift your spirits when you can. If I could, I would have asked someone to play hymns and scriptures and spiritual songs 24-7 for me. I could have listened to someone read to me every day and love it. I am convinced it would have been to my advantage. I wished people would have taken turns to spend fifteen minutes every day, even twice a week to come over and play instruments or sing. I pray earnestly for them that are in bed and ill. Most of them can't even get the words out to ask for these things. They can't even think. I ask God to give families and friends sensitivity to their needs. I know that Morgellons patients are giving up nonetheless. We can only try. These thoughtful deeds may be the answer for many of them. Remember, most of them don't want to wake up the next day. That breaks my heart. I've been there. That kind of dread is so awful. "In all thy ways acknowledge him and he shall direct thy paths" (Proverbs 3:6). If you're taking care of someone with this disease and feel as though you have nothing to give, don't give up. The smallest gestures are huge. Just being in their room, moving about, dusting or vacuuming, is comforting for them. Some may prefer their hand held, a soft song, humming. Know your individual and his/her needs. I'm confident my God will lead me and trust that he will lead you too.

You have to believe good things are ahead. It may seem like forever, but wait. Don't be impulsive. Don't give up. I hope I hear from people that read this. I need encouraging too! Please email me and let me know how things are going. My email address is *bobbi_devine@yahoo.com*. Make sure you put "response" in the subject line. God bless you all. Better days are ahead, my friends. Eat well and get lots of rest patients and caregivers. Getting exhausted makes us want to give up. I pray that you all have strength to get to that light at the end of the tunnel. My heart is so strongly engaged in your well-being! Don't forget, I'm pulling for you.

Chapter Five

As I was attempting to make changes in my small world, I continued examining the endless number of particles coming out of me. I had Morgellons since 2004 and had constant flare-ups, one overlapping another or more! With this steady stream of debris coming out of me, I don't recall seeing the same flare-up twice! Every particle had its own feature. They would last for months at times, yet never returned the same. It was endless. I am reminded of an incident I called the black seeds. I've read that many people with Morgellons get these. They lasted a long time in me, at least a year. As I recall my initial encounter with these, I cringe. I don't know what they were going to do. They didn't dissolve in water. All of them erupted in a thin small sac! Ick. When looked at under a microscope, they appear to have been wrapped in cellophane. I remember going into the basement to take a bunch of them off of my skin. I placed them in an old jar lid. I couldn't stand having anything hanging on me. If I didn't have strength to bathe, I would remove them with a cloth, tweezers, or whatever else worked. At first, I hadn't paid much attention to these little black seeds. But once I started to study them, I could not get comfortable. I couldn't sleep without clean sheets, pajamas, and a bath every night, if possible. Bathing took so much strength, it was so hard, so tiring. It took so much strength to do anything. It felt as if I had weights tied to my arms and legs. It's not possible to be reliable with baths, proper eating or anything else when your as sick as I was. We can only try our best with any help that we have.

When I bathed the bottom of the bath tub would be speckled with so many black seeds. MANY of them . . . all of the time. You never feel clean. So, so creepy! Ugh! Another day of facing this was just too much. I had trouble going to bed at night not knowing what was coming out of me. Knowing that no one could help me was the real fear.

I had a dear friend bring me out of town for a biopsy of a lesion. I was desperate for answers. Will they find something and end this once and for all? The doctor took off a quarter-sized piece of skin approximately one-fourth to one-half inch thick. The good news, no cancer or parasites. Yet, no diagnosis either. That was more than I could handle that day, and of course, I was rushed home and went back to bed.

When I'm at home I always try to keep loose skin particles in a tissue, tray, or the garbage can. Before bed one night, I went around the apartment emptying all the trash. I found that old jar lid with the black seeds in it. The so-called 'sac' that I had told you about had now shrunk into a piece of skin wrapped around the seed like a belt! It now was skin colored and became uniformly wrapped mid-way around the seed. Hmm . . . I was puzzled. As I went thru all of the seeds I was shocked! One of the seeds became large and appeared to have 'legs' sticking up out of the 'skin belt'. Coming out from under the belt was a black shell-like substance. It had an iridescent sheen to it and resembled a beetle, an insect. I was speechless! Didn't the doctor say I had no parasites?! I had called a couple more doctors. They said it was impossible for bugs to be coming out of my skin unless I had been in the rainforest and was infested some how. Even that, according to one, was unlikely. My best thought was about the chemical(s) I had apparently consumed ending up with Morgellons Disease. To the best of my knowledge, some pesticides drive bugs away and some draw them in and it kills them. Was this a real beetle, or debris resembling a bug? Morgellons is known for its earthlike particles and wood-like slivers. I've had mossy growth, burrs, seeds, etc. Maybe the Morgellons did produce this bug-like product. I could only assume that it was possible for the bugs to be drawn to me and may have planted eggs under my loose tissue. Or did they get drawn to the ashtray full of seeds that sat there for a weekend, laying eggs in them? So it was growing but unable to get out of the skin belt, or the pesticide eventually killed it. How awful it is to have a disease that no one knows about. There are no answers, no comfort. I sickened myself! I didn't want to get in my bed. I feared sleeping with this gross debris in my bed. It was frightening. There was no possible way to get comfortable. None! For years! And to top it off, there were ignorant people that actually laughed and bullied me like children. They doubted me and argued with me. I got kicked when I was down. I desperately needed loving words, kindness, and sensitivity. All alone again! Me and my Morgellons. But I'm a fighter.

Chapter Six

Another weapon that I fought endlessly was the thickening of skin. This started the evening that my first sign of Morgellons came (the blisters). To this day, I haven't totally recovered skin-wise. The skin thickening is something else, so much work. You have to daily exfoliate every part of your body and avoid ripping your skin while you're at it. So painful and exhausting, ugh!

Another tiresome task for the weak and weary. Too weak and too weary. I couldn't stop fighting, so I sent a friend to one of those dollar stores to pick up a variety of sponges, washcloths, soaps, and lotions. It was time to get to work. Scrubbing, peeling, picking, shaving, clipping, cutting off thick dead skin . . . exfoliating! Ugh again! I cried daily watching this evil disease chew me up and spit me out from head to toe.

Make good choices on what you use. Do research on products first. Some things can come from dollar stores and department stores. However, the best products I used came from from swansonvitamins.com. Oregano oil kills bacteria and fungus. It is second to garlic for having an antibiotic effect on us. I rubbed it on my skin and took it orally too, daily. There's a lot you can do. I bathed in different salts, clays, apple cider vinegar, baking soda, and epsom salt. They all had a soothing effect on me depending on the type of lesions I had at the time. Some lesions needed neutralizing, and some needed moisturizing, etc. And don't be afraid of scrubbing. I had to use strength that I didn't have. In retrospect, you have to be gentle. You don't want to use too much force with some products like a pumice stone. No unnecessary bleeding! We bleed enough! However, it really is impossible to avoid some bleeding. I hope people will contact me by e-mail and let me know how these ideas help and how they are doing. Bathing is so much better than showering when it comes to that thick skin. When you are done soaking and scrubbing, just spray or shower yourself off. Don't forget the moisturizing when needed either. It does minimize the amount of stuff sloughing off you. Again, depending on the type of flare-up you're having. Olive oil and Eucerin are very good as well. Keep it up. You will feel better. I know you are tired. Keep fighting.

I never signed up for help from sources such as human services. They can do a lot for you. I was too sick to call and arrange that. If you have help, ask them to make contacts for you. You can choose the type of help you get. That will be determined by your condition. Some may want cooking, cleaning, vacuuming, and bathing help. Whatever help you get reserves your strength for other Morgellons chores. I know what you're thinking. This feels like a full-time job. Keep asking and seeking for help as you can. It will make it much easier for you, if easy is such a thing with this cruel disease. Hang in there and don't forget. Rest and sleeping is number one. Call it a night even if it's early. When I was overwhelmed, nothing was so comforting as silence, and I'm sure that knowing someone is there for you would be awesome. Fight for help. Enjoy any little comforts or blessings that you can. We live in a very small world, very painful and dreaded.

Find comfort, my friends. It keeps us stronger and gives us a better attitude, if there can be such a thing with this nasty disease. Don't think of quitting; you can't! Remember, we are warriors. Rest until that flame within you is rekindled. No matter how short that rekindling may be. Keep on keeping on. I'm counting on you, my dear friends.

Chapter Seven

Have you ever felt faint in the sun and heat? I would get limp and unstable on my feet! I also would get blurry vision. I believe it was the summer of 2006 when a police officer pulled me over. I didn't know what I did wrong. Well, he let me know! I had veered to the left considerably then again to the right. He was sincere in telling me I could have hurt myself or someone else. He asked if I had been drinking. I said no. Tears came as I explained my Morgellons to him. He asked me to please park my car and have a loved one pick me up. I was told to no longer drive while the heat was weakening me and my eyesight was poor. That was all summer. My world just got smaller. One more limitation.

I would go for a walk and find myself laying in someone's yard under a tree worried about making it home. I recall riding my bike several times and literally falling over as though I had fainted. I probably did. I learned quickly not to go out into the sun anymore. I got so, so weak. Morgellons and sun/heat don't mix. I'm sure many of you have found that out by now. Stay safe and don't spend time outside especially during the day. It's sad to say . . . but I spent my entire time indoors during the summer. A curse of the "M" word. To be safe, I wouldn't go out of the house between April and September. I immediately felt it, even in an air-conditioned car, as well as inside when I would walk by the windows or open doors. I had to keep my shades drawn and would tape newspaper where small rays of sun would shine in. I felt scared. I felt threatened in the heat. It has something to do with the UV rays and heat combo. Gathering my thoughts about this, again, I believe that all the fibers within me absorbed the fluids in me, and I would immediately get dehydrated in heat or sun. That's my theory.

In Northern Minnesota, for one without Morgellons disease April through September is the only time you can go out without snow and cold. I missed it so badly. A prisoner of Morgellons. While I was in bed ill, my first daughter gave me two darling grandbabies. My heart yearned to be outside with them in the sun, at the beach, in the grass. My heart grieved. I couldn't be the mother and grandmother I so desperately wanted to be. I got so sad whenever I would think of all my inabilities and disabilities. This is huge. Very depressing. The very worst time to have Morgellons is in the warm/hot weather.

As much as I wanted that to change somehow, it didn't. Not until 2013. This was my first normal summer in nine years. Wow, I've come a long, long, restless way. Summer was my favorite season so this problem really upset me. Not all Morgellons sufferers have all the same symptoms. I hope you are spared and don't suffer many. They rob us of so much. I think of a scripture, John 10:10 that says, "The thief comes to steal, kill, and destroy, but I have come to give you life and life abundantly." I pray this prayer for each of you out there in misery. No matter what "the thief" is robbing you of, I pray that God will give it back to you abundantly!

I hadn't seen progress in my heat tolerance. I proceeded to do my Morgellons chores, as I called them. In hopes of getting stronger in any given area, I studied about vitamins and supplements to see what I needed or didn't need. You've probably noticed a change in your vision as well. I've read that Morgellons patients have rapidly decreasing vision. I certainly did. The good news is that your sight will improve significantly as you get stronger. I give credit to diet and supplements for changes like this. My vision became noticeably better. And I give God credit for touching my eyes.

    I woke up one morning, and everything was unusually bright. I was convinced that the landlord changed all the bulbs in the home. Hmm, that didn't sound right. I would've seen him doing it, I thought. I brushed it off, trying to forget about it. I couldn't. I kept checking all the lights. Finally, I asked the landlord, and he said he hadn't changed any. That's when I realized that I had received an unbelievable amount of my vision back. It was wonderful. I went around the house all day, looking at things and watching out the window. It was phenomenal. Things popped out at me! Colors were brighter, images clearer, shiny things shinier. It was a gift, by all means. Just a pleasure. I didn't realize I had lost so much of my sight. It was a gift, a blessing. I had been in bed so many years. I didn't expect good things to happen. After so many years of suffering, you don't expect much else. It was so beautiful. For months, I could not stop pointing out pretty, colorful things. It felt exciting, like a carnival! When I went out walking or to a store, I had to control myself. I felt as though I constantly talked about the colors around me! I was worried about my kids, afraid I may be embarrassing them. I just couldn't help it; I was so thankful. I didn't have anyone to share in the experience with. They didn't understand. That hurt. Nonetheless, I was full of joy in my weakened state. Yes! Nothing could have taken the smile off my face. I'm so humbled, grateful, and blessed that I could share that with you here in this book. I looked forward to the day I could talk to my people about these things. You, my readers, other victims, we understand each other, that is if you've gone through it also. I couldn't wait to tell my story in writing. I couldn't talk to others without them giving me strange looks or even arguing the issues. I pray anyone else going through this will fight so we all can say, "We made it." Stronger every day; stronger every day. Fight and you will be stronger every day. It's so, so slow, but believe it, you are going forward. I am now, after nine plus years, remarkably better. I'm grateful, but I'm also stubborn. I want to feel 100 percent complete! Come on, we can do it!

I didn't have a clue that my hearing was affected as well. The brain fog they say we get consumed me. I was never alert, so lacking in awareness, and always seemed to be alone. I can't finish this chapter without telling you about receiving a great deal of my hearing back. I woke up one morning and went to brush my teeth (this, too, is important: you can lose teeth from this, so brush often!). As I was brushing, I clearly heard children playing outside. It was unusual. I then realized that I hadn't heard that in some time. I was just enjoying it. Back in my room, sitting on the edge of my bed, I heard a choir of birds singing. They were so beautiful! I hadn't heard birds for years but wasn't aware of it till then. I sat there in awe. It sounded like they were singing for me exclusively. I sat smiling, weeping. This shocking new sound kept surprising me for many weeks to come. One day in the dining room, I kept hearing a repetitive bird. I was confused, so I yelled up to my daughter to come and listen. She yelled down, "Mom, that's Dad's cell phone!" We laughed and realized I had a lot to get used to and relearn as well. I listened so closely to all birds. Some seemed tone deaf; others sounded like they forgot words to their songs. It was delightful. This still gets my attention at times. There is a lesson to be learned through that, as the saying goes, "Stop and smell the roses" or in my case "Stop and hear the birds!" So my hearing became sharper, and I trust yours will too. Good things will happen again. Believe. Sufferers, fighters . . . believe.

It's almost impossible to see anything good when sick with Morgellons. Nothing seems good. It's a curse, for sure. Devastating.

To end this chapter, I want to give you a list of herbal supplements my dear friend Al had recommended from Carnicom as well as other websites and radio stations. As he studies, he keeps up on the latest info for me. Here's the list. The amounts I take could be different from what you should take. I recommend researching it on CarnicomInstitute.org.

1. Oregano oil gel caps
2. Oregano oil liquid for skin
3. Buffered vitamin C
4. B-complex
5. Calcium
6. Magnesium
7. Potassium
8. Iodine
9. Peppermint soaps, lotions, and essential oils
10. Thieves oil

Chapter Eight

The weapons of Morgellons are the lesions, how they are formed and transformed, and how they attack and spread. I personally named them weapons because they all have their own ammunition to extend their misery. Many people get breakouts from the waist down or just on their face, neck, arms, or maybe all over. Mine ended up to be all over, from head to toe. Everyone is different. It tries to get on my face, but I try to use some type of minty face wash. As I mentioned earlier, Morgellons doesn't like to hang out where it's minty or has camphor, mentholatum, eucalyptus, and the like. So you can protect some areas of the skin to prevent scarring. You have to care for your skin like clockwork. You can't miss a beat. If you have people helping you, ask them to remind you to do your Morgellons chores, your routine cleansing.

Someone told me to keep notes of everything to remind myself. Wrong! I would either lose the notes or forget that I wrote them. So use the help that you have. Things will change! Oh yes, it's ever so slowly. But you will see change. That is our goal—to stay on top of this monster, to win the fight. We need to "one-up" this disease so we can be in control. Hopefully all signs of it will stop, never to return. This is my prayer for myself and you all!

So let's get back to things I found out about as I studied my skin. I hope I do not neglect to mention some of the important things of the past. Like I said, I was affected in 2003, so it's been many years. I do recall one of the first ugly objects I saw. It looked like a worm. Oh no, it's not a parasite. In fact, when I took a closer look at it, it was a piece of skin tissue the size of a match and the length varied. It also was red. Maybe blood, maybe not. They always were attached to me by one end of it. It was a part of my affected flesh for sure. I hated them. They were so creepy looking! These were very slick/slippery but would come off with a tweezers. I recall pulling at least six of them off; balled up it was the size of a cotton ball. I placed them on a tissue. Literally, in a matter of a second or two, it shrunk, dried up to the size of a small, very fine fiber. It no longer resembled the particle that was on me. These pathetic things were always circling the edge of a lesion. Some lesions had a couple of them around them, others had more. They lasted for about a year. The particles appear to run a course and transform into something different but just as wicked. Some came and went for a year or so then quit. I never knew how to care for these "red worms." I was using the oregano oil on them. I would pop a gel cap with a needle if I was out of the liquid. Same thing. I would then squeeze the gel caps on these ugly pieces of, ugh, me. I rubbed it in slightly and covered it. Some of this stuff was difficult to look at or think of. I tried hard to forget about them. Impossible! I was forced to see them 24-7. I was a living, walking piece of Morgellons. I lost sleep over it all the time. I lost all peace of mind. I no longer felt like I was a part of life. I was sitting on the bench, watching others live. How long could I do this? Can I really keep this up? My world consists of four walls. I've been so socially affected. It became hard to talk to people or go anywhere. I could no longer relate to the average human being. I had a secret and needed to tell someone. Yet anytime I made an effort to do so, I clearly sensed rejection and doubt. I'd get strange looks. Usually, it put distance between me and others, which was fine with me. At this point, peace meant being alone.

I had many experiences that made me want to run away and escape. Where would I go? I couldn't leave my body! My body was my enemy, my prison. I had to live and sleep in it. An unspeakable feeling. I saw too much, too many strange and peculiar things. I knew too much that no one else knew. I want to be normal again so badly!

One particular incident I recall was in my apartment's basement. I noticed some fibers coming out of the top of my hands. They were flesh colored and had a smooth texture. The crazy pattern of breaking out relentlessly continues. As they came out, they looked thick like yarn. They coiled up as they grew longer. Each turn of the coil would fuse to my hand. I appeared to have curly noodles atop of my hand! Oh my god, please, I want to faint now. I want to wake up when this goes away. I sat motionless, waiting for my daughter to come home from school. I had to show her this to be a witness for me. It took her longer than normal to get home. As I waited, the "noodles" started to retract. Yes, they started to go back into my skin. What word can describe this ungodly, gross sight? Fear of myself was starting to set in. Ick. My daughter walked in; I quickly showed her. I then scraped every piece of this evil off. Never did I see that one again. I curled up lying on an afghan, crying. Who am I? What am I? No one will listen. I need a hug so badly. I need love to feel accepted and okay. I felt like an empty shell as I lay there crying. I had no place of solace or refuge. I've never been in this place or heard of it. Nobody but me and others with this disease. As

I began falling asleep, I regretfully hoped once again that I wouldn't wake up.

As I began to reveal more of my battles with Morgellons, I developed another unusual flare-up. One of these flare-ups has to be the last one. I'll be healed or die from it. Unfortunately, I had to live through yet another. I've heard of other Morgellons sufferers complain of this. I'm assuming it's common yet no less frightening. If I didn't know anything of this affliction, I would have wrote this off as dry skin.

A person unfamiliar with the symptoms wouldn't have noticed it. I called it fudgy skin. What happens is this: my skin becomes very soft looking. It looks relatively smooth, not a lot of swelling or infection. Yet the skin will very slightly break open (barely visible to the naked eye), and it begins to push out what I call white flags. It's a very small diamond-shaped particle. It's not dry at all. This is where someone could mistake it for dry skin. It's not dry at all. It's very white. If you have a cut, lesion, or blister, they will come out of them in volumes periodically. I found out that these innocent-looking specks were as evil as any other symptom. They are "ammunition." They don't come from any one area. They come from any area. It was very uncomfortable as I went through this. It was unexpected, and I could rarely take control of it. The major problem with these particles is that they immediately reabsorb into your skin once they are loosened and no longer remain in the area they came out of. There are other objects that do this as well, but for now, we will paint this picture as accurately as we can. When I first had these, I quickly picked each one up from my skin, moving fast so they wouldn't reabsorb. I'd pinch up to twenty of them and wipe them off with a tissue. By the time I reached the tissue, they had sunk into my fingertips. I could pull them off if I was fast enough, but I normally couldn't keep up the pace. After a while, I felt like a tree frog! My fingertips had fresh round calluses on them. They had little feeling, like any callus does. If you peeled them off, you would risk dropping a piece on your arm, leg, wherever, and the entire process would begin again, as it would absorb into those areas as well. This, by all means, is a wicked weapon. It literally falls on your skin and sinks in. This would remind me of going to the lake with my dad as a kid. We'd skip rocks, and along the top of the water, the rock would skip a time or two then sink. That's my analogy. If the white flags that came off you were big enough, you could see the image of it as it sunk. Now I want someone to tell me that is normal. Whenever my skin was "fudgy," it made me nervous, because I knew that any loose piece of skin, dry blood, tar-like particles, etc., would sink into me. It wasn't just the white flags anymore.

 I had a girlfriend over one day and was showing her the unbelievable things going on with my skin. She was very comforting and realistic about what was going on. She saw it and knew it was really happening. I showed her what can happen with this type of skin. I pushed down on an open sore atop of my hand. With my other fingers, I pulled skin from the left and right. I covered the sore with this skin and sealed it, hiding the sore underneath the fudgy skin. I then gently rubbed the seam of skin where I pulled it together. The seam disappeared. No one would have ever known that there was a large sore beneath the top layer of skin. I stayed strong and held on. I was not going to snap or let anyone call me delusional. I had a witness. I was on a mission. Wherever this inhumane condition was derived from was evil. Who could allow something like this to happen to their own people? Or was it merely accidental? I knew this wasn't natural but a manmade chemical. It was made to torment its victims obviously. One day I believe we will know the true cause of this, its purpose and intention. We deserve to know the truth.

Many reports have been consistent in sugarcoating this affliction, blowing it off as something minor. I'm not alone in this battle; I'm giving it my all. I challenge them that say it's minor to visit the sick! I am living the facts and writing the truth. I will pass the test.

As I reach the end of this "white flag" issue, I have no answers. I will always grab VapoRub when all else fails. In this case, anything moist only helps it adhere to everything you touch. I'll put on mentholatum talcum powder. Then, on top of that, when it's dried out a bit, I put on calamine lotion. I'd love to know if anyone out there has advice themselves. Thank you, people, you are all so dear to me. We need each other. Reach out to family members of the sick! We don't need criticism but to be encouraged, informed, and directed. Keep it up! Keep going strong. I'll have you in my prayers. Everyone out there suffering, you are so important. I wish I could comfort you and your families.

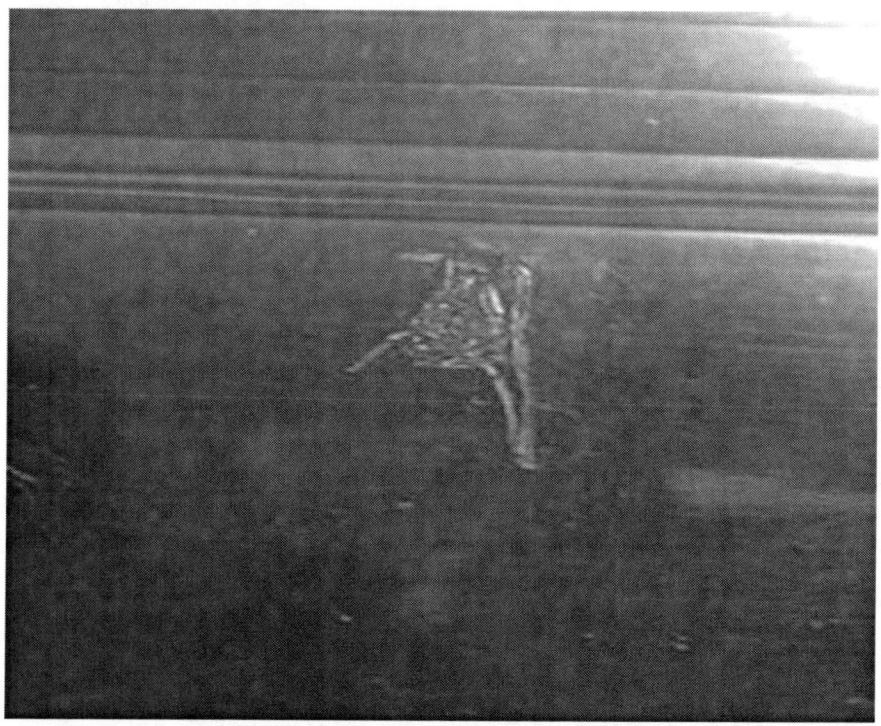

This specimen came off my leg when I had scratched it. It initially was a round gelatinous ball. Once I held on to it, it became like a ball of yarn, so to speak. It started to unravel. I placed it in this baggie.

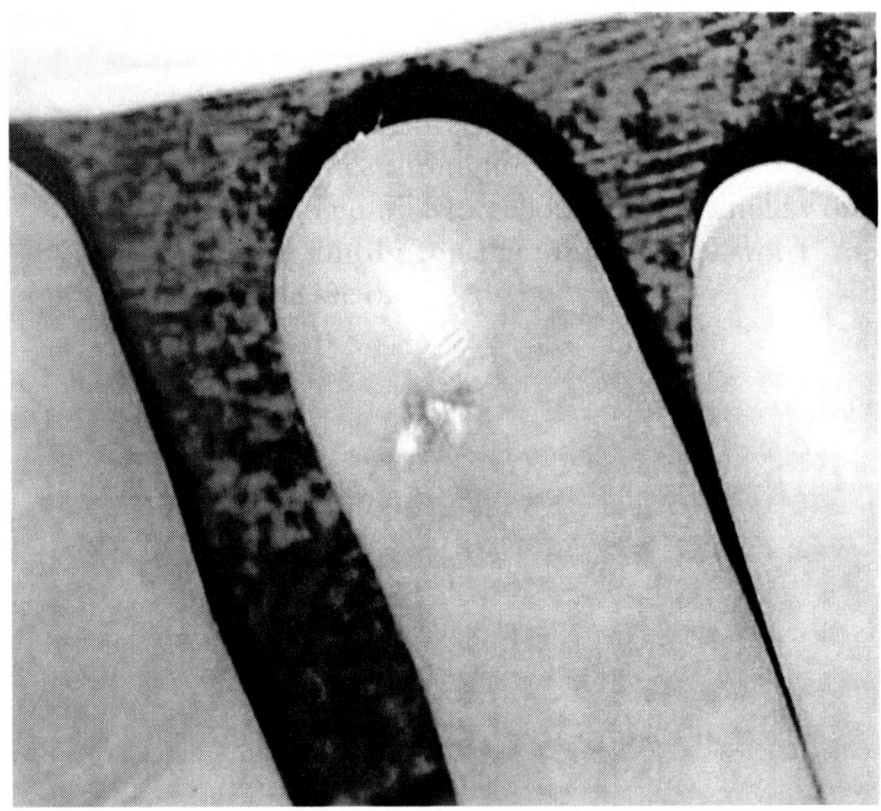

This is the infamous fibers in a basic blue. When I hold them, they remain blue, often times changing shades of blue. When I put them down on something, they turn white or grayish.

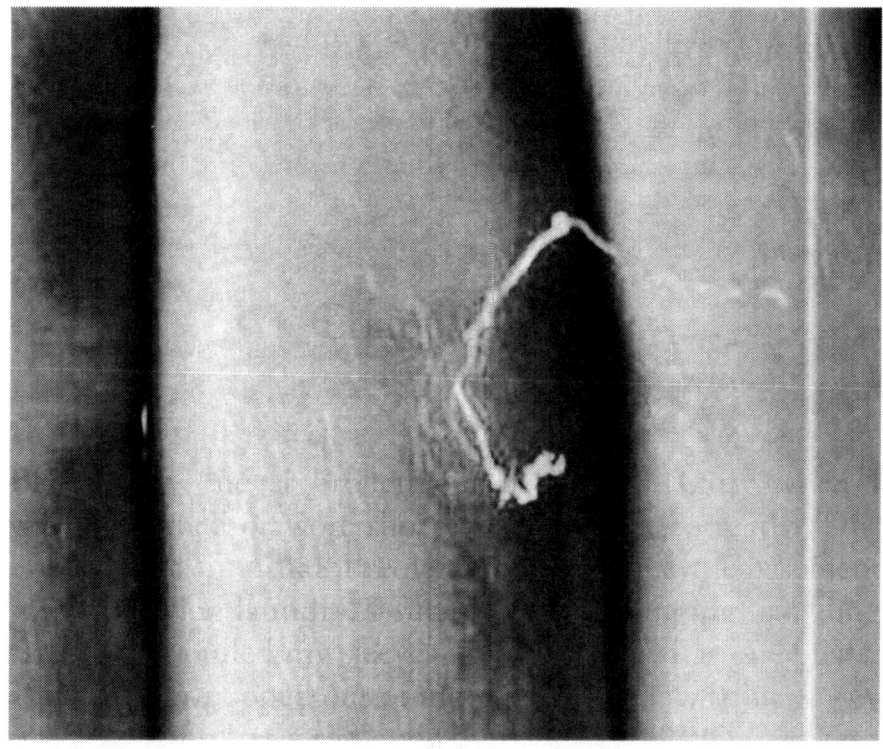

This object is a classic gold tinsel, so I called it. It comes in different forms. One of the other formations is gold splinters.

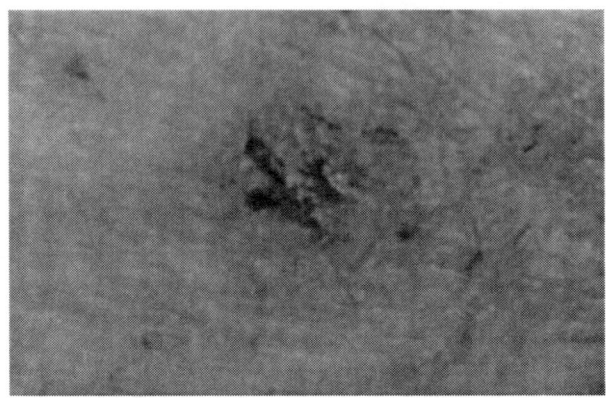

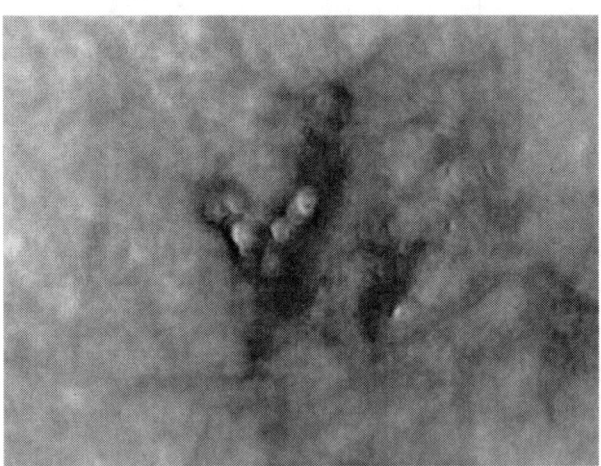

Here we have the black tarry substance. When it's ready to fall off, it develops an iridescent sheen to it. That sheen remains on it when it dries.

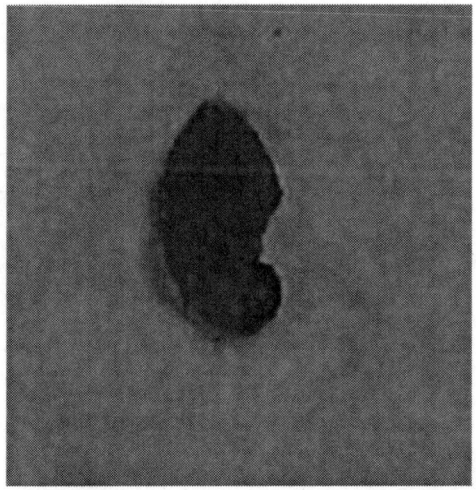

In this photo I have a "black seed." There are so many of these throughout the course of the disease. I found them in large numbers in my bed and in the bottom of the bathtub after the water was drained. They are often found with a sac around them. It's very thin, like a covering of a blister. It isn't always noticed. If left alone to dry, the particles take on the shape of beetle wings, legs or otherwise. I've *never* seen a bug in my skin; however, the particles oftentimes will dry up and resemble dirt, grass, or insects.

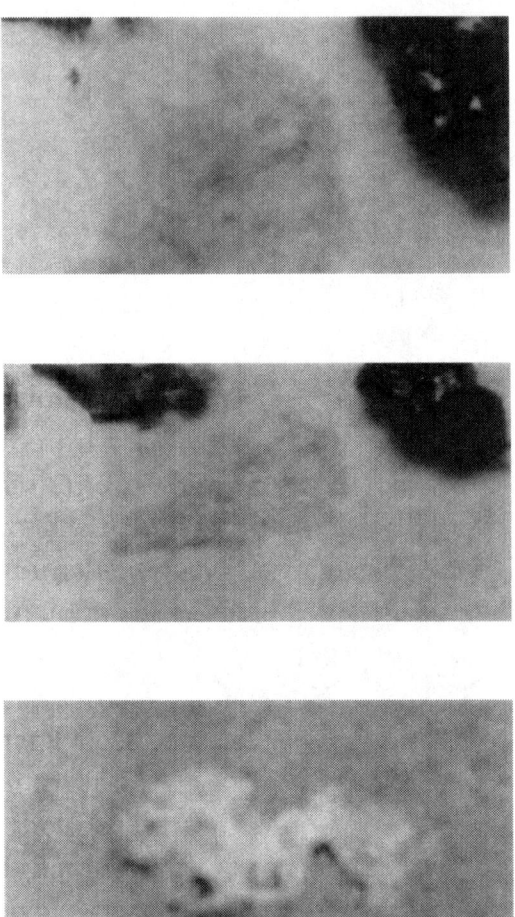

These snapshots were hard to get. They aren't the best quality but well enough to show the detail. Oftentimes skin would peel off me like hangnails. When it came off and dried, it looked like these in the photos, resembling ribbons and coiled. Many would look like Swiss cheese.

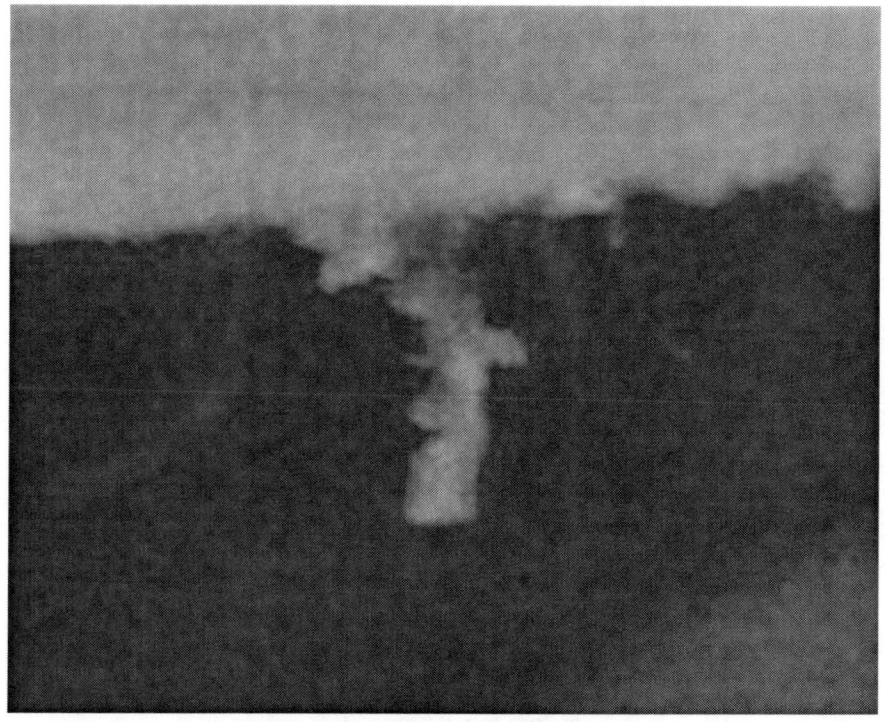

This is a rare picture of a specimen still in my skin, working its way out. The small round things stuck on it are beads, often found strung together. They break up into small pieces that re-infect you and spread the lesions all over.

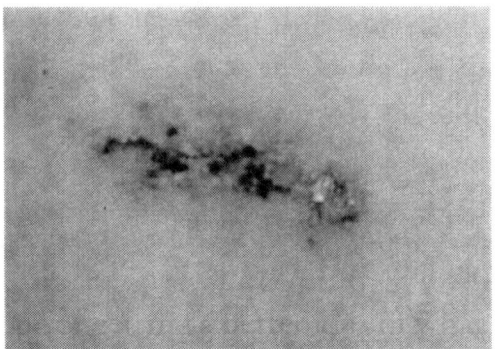

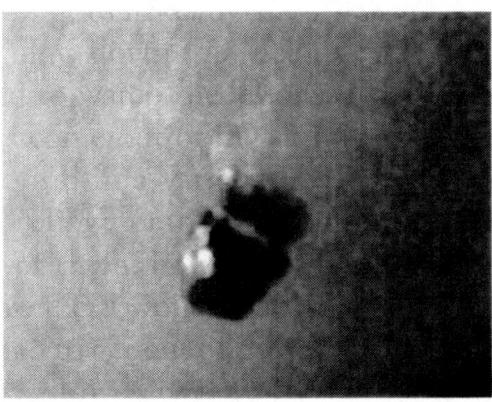

The top picture is a UV still in my skin. They light up and look like they have a little battery in them. The other two photos are UVs at different stages. One has a tarry substance on it. Also, notice the beads on them.

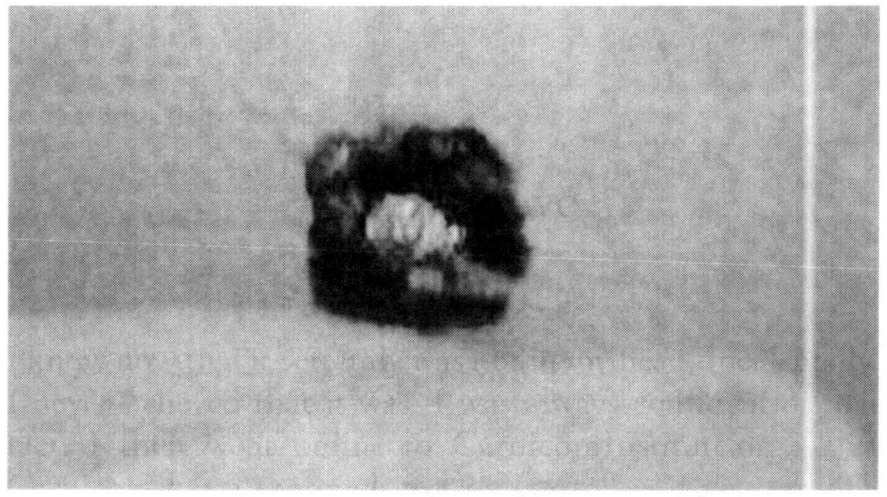

This tarry substance has a ball of stringy "metal" in the middle.

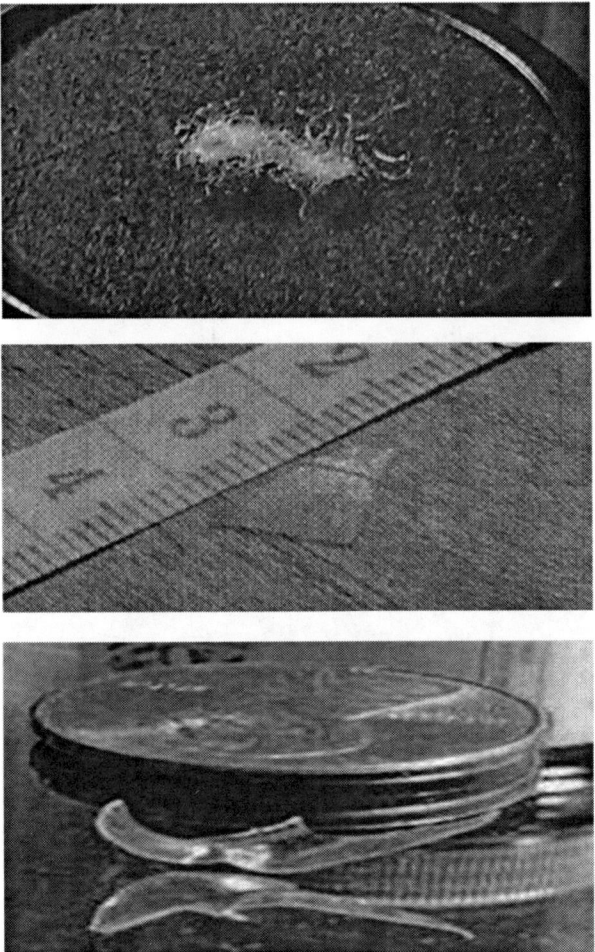

These three pics are stages of the fibers transforming into the blue transparent piece of plastic. These fibers consumed me. It was my last flare-up. I had difficulty breathing because they were in the air so thick. I couldn't dust or vacuum enough. I literally had a handful of them in one batch of clothes when I did laundry. They had bunched up in my sock and meld/melted together from my body heat. That is the second image. I then held it on my fingertip, and in twenty minutes, it had shrunk and became the third image, a strong guitar pick-like piece of plastic.

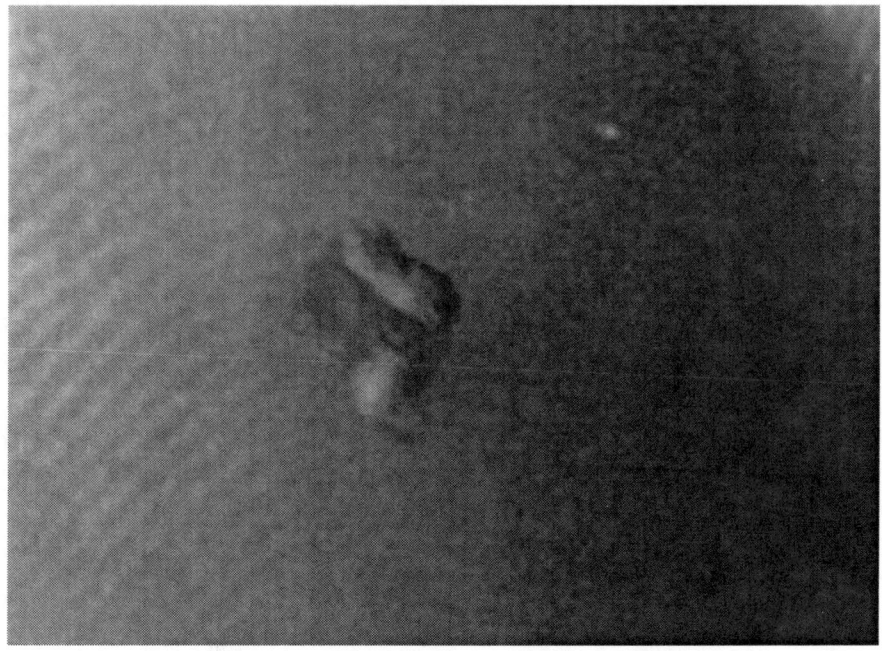

This particle would flake off me and look like ordinary skin. When it dried, it developed the texture of grass or wheat. The color would vary from gold to green. This one was like a leaf. Most of them had the appearance of a blade of grass.

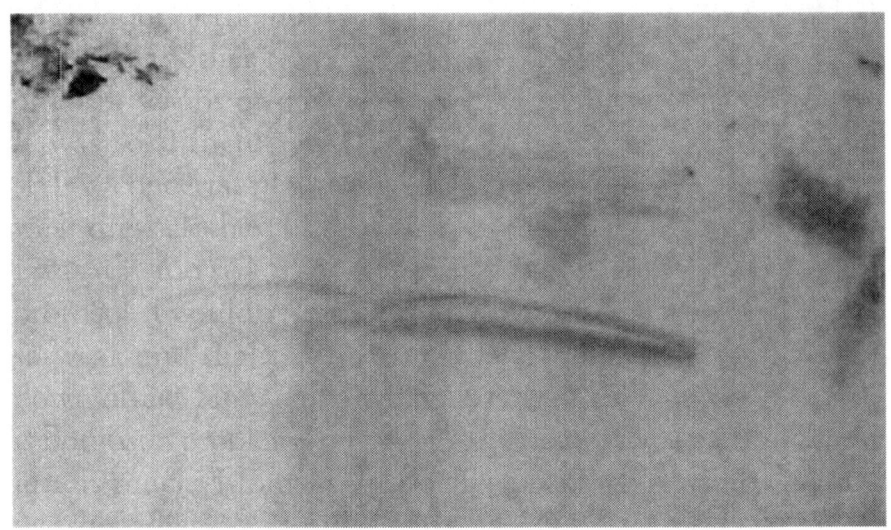

It was common for fibers to dry up and then have a stronger, thicker fiber protrude from it. This image is an example of that.

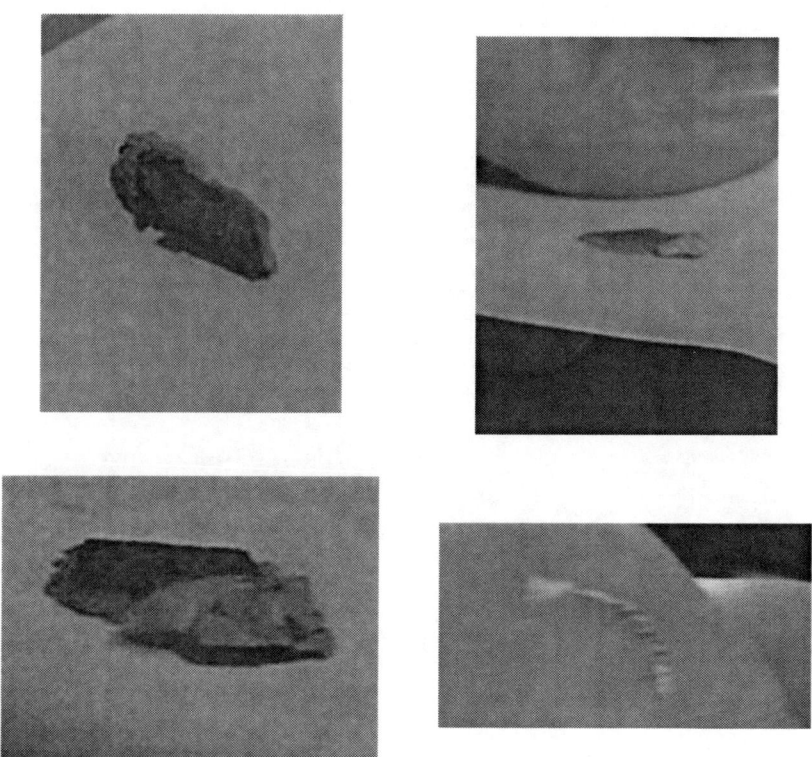

This indeed was a hangnail, approximately one-quarter inch long. This is what happened to it as it dried up and transformed! How ugly! You can see the underlying tissue on the bottom. The red stuff is not blood but a secretion similar to red soda. It has the fibers, beads, and the grassy, earthy things.

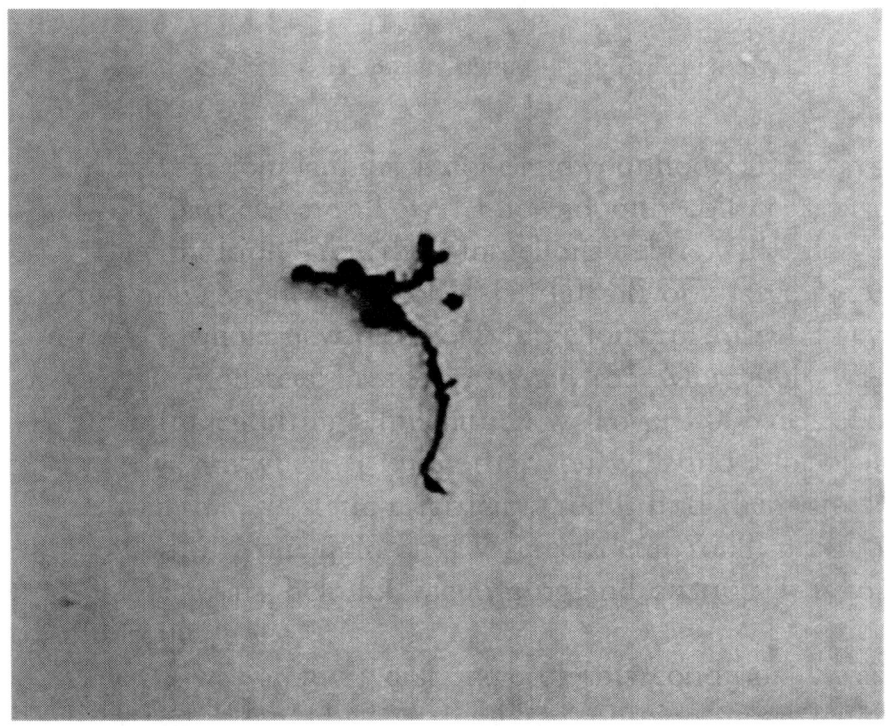

This is debris from my lesions that appeared often. Initially I thought it was something I dragged in from outside. It appears and feels like a small branch off a raspberry plant or something of the like. It felt like it and looked like it. They were very sharp and painful. After studying them over a period of time, I realized they were an accumulation of stuff coming out of my lesions. They formed with the friction of my skin and clothes. I found them stuck in my clothing and linens. They were all over.

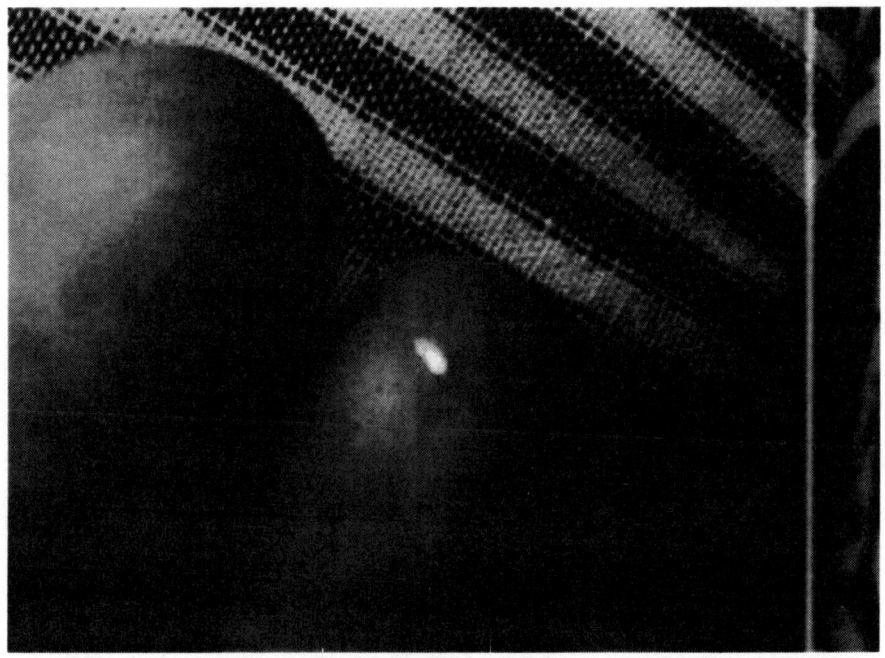

This is one of the many metal slivers I pulled out of my skin. They were small, shiny and did considerable damage. I frequently developed infections when these were present. I believe they would occasionally get stuck in me while trying to come out of my skin. This created abscesses, infections that had to be treated with the antibiotic Bactrim.

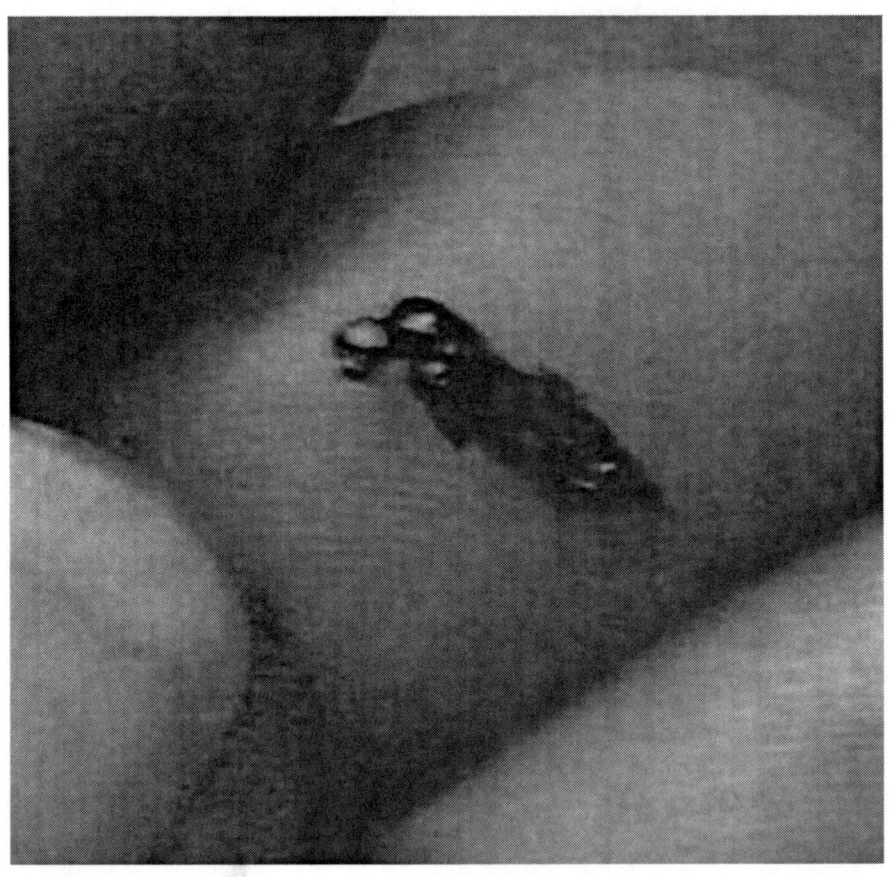

The threatening beads came out in this tarry substance.

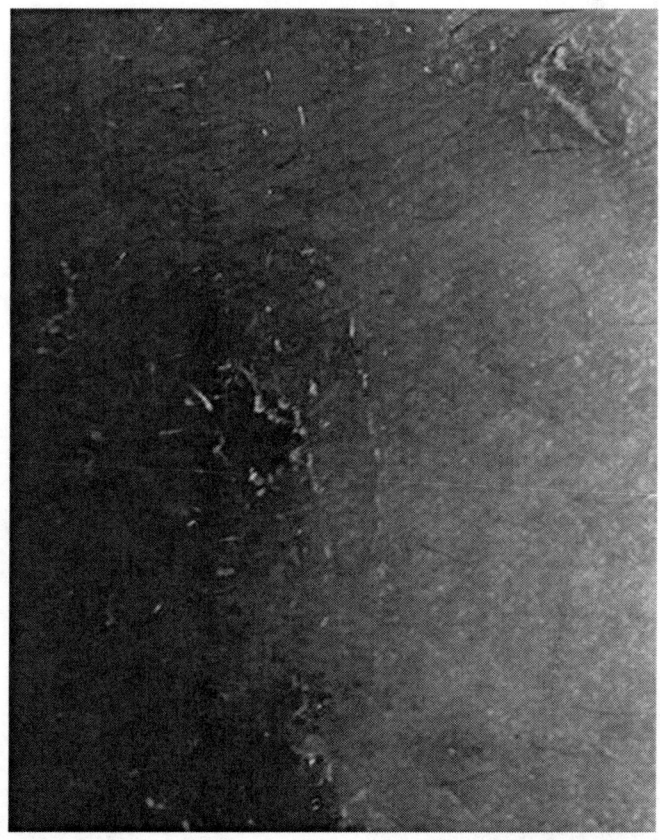

A small area of one of my arms. Several lesions are on it. It's swollen and very painful. It also oozed out debris constantly. You couldn't ignore it for a minute or the stuff would be all over everything. It was work to keep up with it the best I could. What a horrible memory.

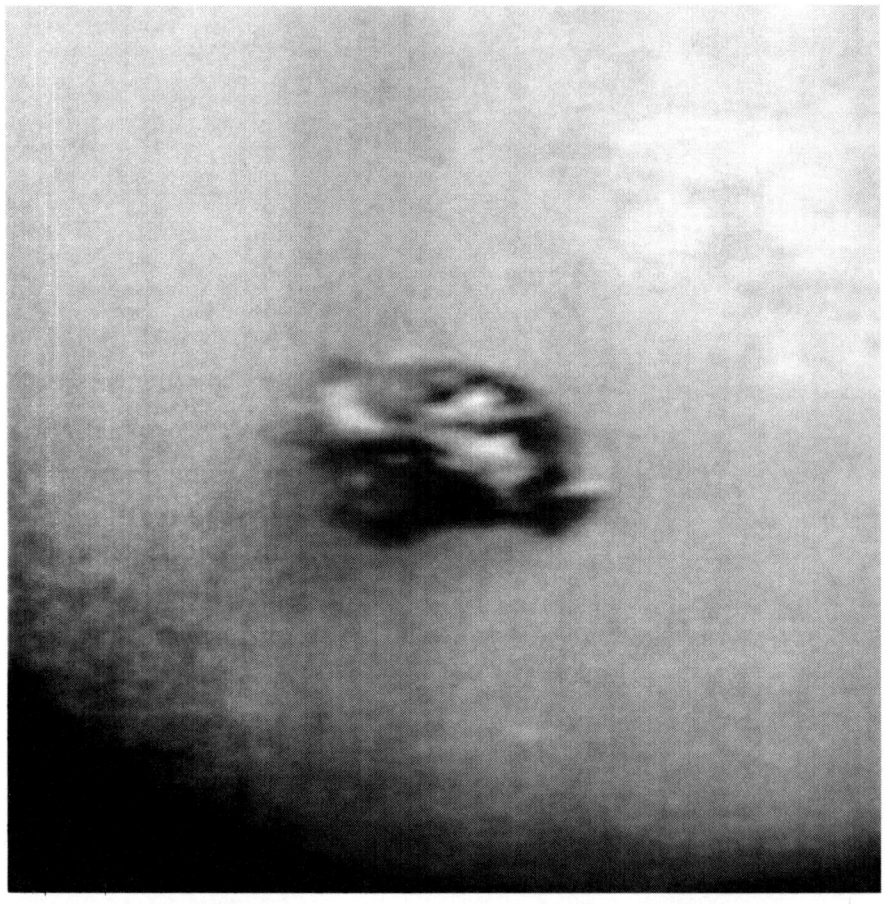

Although my photos are poor quality, I felt they were significant. This one shows the combination of earthy, tarry, and white fibers.

Chapter Nine

Of course you had an idea that when you purchased this book it wasn't going to be pleasant. But I'm determined to share with you all the darkness I experienced, along with the hope. My hope is to give you some information no matter how large or small to make your journey easier than mine was.

You would think that after years of seeing this stuff and this strange activity, I would be used to it. Not at all. They repulse me as though I had just seen them for the first time.

Well, I must tell you the next few experiences no matter how difficult it may be. Even though I've struggled at the thought of exposing them, I know I shouldn't keep anything to myself. These are just as important as the other particles, if not more. What makes them so important is the time and patience it took to tone down the attacks. I did learn how to and was able to calm these nasty storms, if you will.

The web is what I called this ugly, dirty debris that sprayed out of me or off me. I didn't study it for long due to the fact that I was very ill when I had it. They were just like a thin spider web. Barely visible. They came out of broken skin, a skin tear, a lesion, or just the smallest break in my skin. I was putting a dressing on an area of my skin when I saw it spray out of one small pore. It sprayed like an aerosol can however, when it came out it didn't separate into a mist.

Although it looked misty, it clung together in strings. Three or four strings would come out at one time. It was as though they were wrapped in a tight coil then released. Each coil went in its own direction. When it landed on my skin every one-eighth inch of it penetrated me. These also looked like a seamstress had finely topstitched my skin. This stuff is acting the same as the fluid I had coming out of me. I wanted to take a picture of this so badly, but each incident didn't last long enough. Like I said, I was so sick; photos did not always enter my mind. I was really puzzled about this one. I took a tweezers and pin and pulled a piece of it out of my skin, the ones penetrating my flesh. When I looked at them under a magnification, they looked like small fish hooks. There was no way of getting these out. All I could do was try to figure out a way to prevent them from either spraying or being able to soak into my otherwise healthier skin. I attempted to use all types of greasy stuff, hoping these "fish hooks" wouldn't be able to grasp my skin. Hmmm . . . it wasn't working. The spray could reach a foot or two depending on your body's position at the time. If you're standing up, it will fall down to your hips, knees, and maybe more.

 I recall standing in the kitchen with a friend when I saw this stuff spray from my shoulder to my thigh. It was next to impossible to wash off. In fact, most of it instigated new lesions. It would wrap around my fingers. I couldn't always see it, but I could feel it. It was really sticky, making my fingers stick together at times and attracting dirt all the time. I never knew how to clean up after this stuff. I used a fingernail brush. It wasn't cleaning well. I had to let it run its course and suffer with the horrible stuff.

 It was hard to breathe during this flare-up. I felt as though I was being wrapped up in a cocoon. A person simply cannot be around other people for any length of time and feel normal.

Normal was a long-lost feeling I yearned to have. I yearned to feel. I yearned to heal. Would I?

My worst encounter was a substance similar to the web; it was frightening. I truly felt as though I was living a horror movie. This flare-up played like a video game and I fought to win, one on one. I had to think and I had to think fast.

I was in bed again for some time, very ill as usual. I noticed a few nickel and dime-sized skin openings on me. As I watched, I saw an area become darker than the rest of my skin. It pulled really tight and had a bumpy texture all its own. I'd say it was approximately as large as a 50 cent piece, with three small black squares and one black rectangle in it. I saw a small drop of fluid. I watched it run down my wrist. As it flowed, it ate a "ditch" in my arm. I would dab it with a tissue. That didn't stop it. Putting pressure on it for quite a while helped, yet when I let go, it proceeded to flow again. I remembered the liquid bandage. I grabbed it and started to put a coat on the intrusive area where the fluid started to seep out. After several layers of this, drying in between, it stopped. There were small blisters underneath, but that was it. Or so I thought. Well, that all came from the rectangular part. Now that the rectangle was covered, the squares started squirting this fluid! I panicked. I had to win this war. I kept telling myself not to give up. I had to stop this monster. I had to know I could defeat this type of activity. Again, I grabbed the liquid bandage and began my struggle to keep the area dry long enough to put the liquid on it and keep doing this until it stops. I was exhausted at this point. This stuff was on a mission and didn't appear to tire. I had several layers on it but was convinced I couldn't put enough on this. Hours went by, and hallelujah, it was dry and stable! Oh my gosh. I was beside myself and needed some rest. Before I had a chance to rest, I saw five holes open up around the entire area that was bandaged with that liquid. It looked like open pores, large ones. As I watched, they too began to spray this fluid. I was under attack. This was no joke. I had no camera or camcorder available. I put my palm on it and pressed down for quite a while with intense pressure for about twenty to thirty minutes. That was long enough to control and bandage it. How long is this going to go on? Can't anyone help me? Think, Bobbi. Think. I was alone. Alone in my room with no one, not a soul to explain any of this to me or to comfort me. I'm really not alone. I know God is with me. He is my source of comfort.

Thinking the end of that flare-up was over, I went to put a white gauze roll around my wrist and went to sleep. I once again was shocked and in disbelief. Under all the layers of liquid bandage, in the holes that the spray and fluid came out of, were one-eighth- to one-fourth-inch black pieces. It looked like a small end of a barbell was stuck in each hole. The other end was up in the air, touching my bandage work. These black things relentlessly went up and down. It appeared that they were fighting for air, fighting to pierce a hole in the bandage that was suffocating it. I was completely and utterly sickened. I used two bottles of the liquid and covered an entire six-by-six-inch area with it. Daily I would do my best not to get this area wet. I certainly didn't want it to get air, so I would put a layer of the liquid bandage on it daily. The entire area was shrinking smaller every day. At the end of two weeks, it had shrunk to under an inch and disappeared. Never to return. Oh my God, what a battle. I had these before but didn't realize their function. Before this happened, I was cutting these areas off with a box cutter, saving them in plastic zipped baggies. I wanted to find these things and examine them. I did find them in a box. This was a nightmare. I wish none of it was true. Well it is and it isn't a delusion. If I didn't have them all in baggies labeled and filed, I probably would think I was crazy! No, I wasn't crazy. This is for real.

Well I found three baggies with the identical lesion in them. They had turned dark brown. One bag was slightly loose. As I examined it I saw that the "black barbells" had poked holes in the plastic! Each piece in the baggie had penetrated a hole through it. The second bag I looked at was airtight. I was unable to shake it around at all. Should I open it? God knows. I looked closer, and the black barbells were lying on top of the pores they came out of. There were no holes in this bag! The plastic bag was too thick and strong for this bunch to pierce it. It looked as though these pieces fought for their lives and lost. Exhausted. Were they still alive? Any of them? Ugh! I couldn't live with myself. Once again, I ran to the clinic as though they were going to help me. I was relieved that they did a biopsy on them and found nothing similar to a parasite, etc. I was given a relatively clean bill of health, just picking they said. Oh my gosh, really? After all I'd been through . . . *really*?

Al stopped by to visit as always. He had been at the library on the computers, researching Morgellons. He came to tell me that Morgellons is not just a pesticide but also robotic! They believe it has an inner battery. After all my unusual flare-ups, I totally believed this.

As time went on, I had a new flare-up again. I was getting so tired. These are called wires. I can't tell you how painful they were. Yes, they were coming out of my skin, thick and black! Once they were out, they became thin and pliable. This was the worst pain I had felt with this disorder. It was unbearable.

The first two to three years was brutal pain. I forgot how it felt. I was angry that I didn't recognize the fact that I was better for a while. No matter how small the change was, there's a need to see it. It's encouraging, small but nonetheless encouraging.

I simply could not move. It felt as though I had literal pins in me. If I moved ever so slightly, they would prick me. After several days, I had a bundle of these in my wrist. It felt like a golf ball-sized metal object that a person scrubs pots and pans with. I no longer could endure the pain. I was weak and started to buckle and fall to my knees. I was helped to bed and stayed there until the following morning. I went to the doctor, realizing I was fainting from the pain. They sent me home with antibiotics but no pain medicine. I had stopped the pain medication and they didn't want me to start it again. "But I'm fainting from the pain", I thought. Regardless, I had a big cross to bear and I needed to keep focused.

Chapter Ten

There are too many diverse particles to write about. I'll just touch on a few briefly, or this will become very long and somewhat repetitive. A very interesting object that I handled was called UVs. They glowed just like the bracelets kids wore at parades. Some of them would even shine a bit at night. It really was fascinating yet, nonetheless, creepy. I did get pictures of these as well. They were typical lesions that spread when released onto your skin. So devastating. They come out in bright colors.

My brain fog was horrible. It caused so many problems for me. I couldn't remember five minutes ago at the worst time of my disease. This is why I couldn't cook or do anything else. I'd forget what I started. I drove to the store one night and got lost coming home. I pulled over and sat on the curb, and I bawled my eyes out. When I looked up, my house was two blocks away. Morgellons diminishes your senses tremendously. You become completely out of touch for long periods of time. This is where we lose so much. If I was well enough to go to a school function for my daughters, I wouldn't remember being there. I begged God for change.

Through all this, I continuously had fibers. They came in all sorts of thicknesses and colors. There was apparently something emitting from my skin that wasn't normal, because when I would touch a fly or a beetle, it would turn colors and become iridescent. When bugs were alive, it would kill some of them. The fibers were interesting. When I held them, they would spread and lengthen. When I put them down, they would stop. When I rolled the fibers into small lint balls, they would separate on their own into two sections. One was colored, and one was usually white. I'm guessing that the real Morgellons fibers were mixed with everyday household lint, and that was the separation. Some of the changes that these particles made were drastic. I supplied photos for you all to get an idea of what I've written.

I'm humbled to be writing this segment of my story to all of you. I'd been engulfed with fear for so long. I was tired and weary.

I knew had I stayed in Minnesota much longer, I would die. It was time. Defeat surrounded me. Living alone was not working for me at this stage in my illness. Death was knocking at my door. It was something I'd never felt before. It was bigger than me. It was Goliath, and I wasn't David. I knew my time was all over with. Yet what did that mean? What was my next step? The phone rang. It was my family in North Carolina. They offered to fly me there and put me up with hope of a new beginning. I knew I had to go. This was a chance to live. Staying back meant death and dying. I was confident of that.

Within days, I had given all my furniture and belongings away. I stored my sentimental items. Then I threw away the rest. This was a fresh start. A new beginning.

North Carolina was a difficult trip. What confusion. First, the heat was damaging to my condition. I became worse. It affected everything from my skin, my emotions, and mind. I was paralyzed with pain, fear and sickness and couldn't do a thing about it. Of course, the people I was staying with didn't know a thing about Morgellons. When they read about it, like most people, they developed an opinion about it that one couldn't change. They never saw the pain, the confusion and the anguish I was in. I don't even remember much except that I was alone all the time. I felt like an outcast. Lost and nowhere to go. I deserved to end it all and it was time I thought. Through it all, I was still in a tug-of-war for my life. "You're going to get through this" was a daily thought. Yet looking at myself caused me to fall into a deep depression. If only I could talk to other victims. If only I could overcome this so I'd be strong enough to help others. With faith, I could pray. With depression, I sought to hurt myself. I searched for places to go and get assisted suicide. I would have to do it myself. I was too sick to make arrangements without help. I kept waking up. I failed at suicide! Was it not my time? Or did I simply not have the necessary tools to complete the job? God only knows.

With despair, I continued to barely thrive. My daughter called me from Minnesota and asked me to come live with her. She offered to help me in any way possible, and she did. She cooked delicious meals daily and brought them to my room. Her husband was generous with the little time he had as well. He saw to it that my room was comfortable. He ran to the store for me and they both bought me things unexpectedly! That made my day! I never felt so needed or important through all this until they started to pay attention to me! This is so important for family and friends to know. Our self-esteem is hardly there. Our sense of belonging is barely hanging on. We are unproductive. We are on a downward spiral. To get attention was huge. I started to thrive for the first time in years. I made doctors appointments and kept them. I could see me developing a strength I'd never seen while suffering with this condition.

Chapter Eleven

I then had an unexpected new flare-up. This scared me to death. It was truly unexpected, I was shocked. It was small white/transparent fibers, and they came out by the thousands or more. They resembled fishing line. I couldn't breathe; they were all over. When I moved, I would see them floating around me. I vacuumed twice daily. I developed a routine. Barely having strength to do it, but I did—washing my clothes after one wear, changing my clothes two to four times a day, lying on my sheets *one* time before washing them. Having a queen-sized bed, I would sleep on each side, then put the top sheet down and do it again before I washed them. It was exhausting. I even vacuumed my walls and belongings. Everything was fluffy! This really got me upset, because I believed I was going to get well soon then this occurred. These fibers would bunch up in areas under my skin. One example I'll give you is my socks. I found a ball of this in one area by my ankle. Checking the other ankle, I found a piece of Scotch tape. Hmmm. I wondered. When did I use tape? It was in perfect condition. I was puzzled. As I thought about it, I was holding the tape. I looked down, and it had shrunk to half the size! I then looked at it closer and realized it was the white fibers. They had flattened out with my body heat and movement. As it flattened out, the heat melded it together. I watched it for approximately forty-five minutes. By then, it had become the size of a small guitar pick. It was football-shaped and now translucent blue. It had the strength of a thin guitar pick. It resembled the plastic particles that would push through my skin, popping out and holding the exact shape of a pick. Those I named guitar picks, and they were a solid cream color. When they came out, they didn't change shape or color, which was unusual. The majority of Morgellons debris did change shape, size, color, and/or texture. I prayed with my heart and soul. God, please stop this! I can't take it anymore. I'm afraid of going back into my "fail to thrive" mode. This went on for two to three months, and as I prayed diligently, I saw it disappear. For months, my skin was peeling and flaking, as though it was getting rid of the leftover Morgellons. And it was.

    I had never remembered feeling so clean. It was sweet! My hair got its normal texture back. I could chew food again without pain. I could wear my clothes more than once! My sheets didn't have to be constantly changed. I'm becoming a new me.

Chapter Twelve

New Chapter: New Me

New me is such a simple and complex problem at the same time. I wept so often at the thought of having a second chance. I was in shock. I had a second chance and I was terrified! Communication with people was so difficult. I prevented it. I realized how sick I had been. It became overwhelming. I reached a point that made me ask, "Why did I want healing?" Difficulty in the healing process did not occur to me. After almost ten years of being semi-comatose, locked out of the world, I came back. Now what?

I sat there and looked around. The colors seemed so vivid. The noises were prevalent. Everything was noticed and seemed larger than life. It seemed loud when I was alone. The fog over my eyes and ears lifted. I would sit and try to identify sounds. Their was so much to take in.

I couldn't go outside. It felt like going to a carnival—too much color, movement and noise. I could only handle small doses of it. I got out of bed every day. This was so rare that even when I was well, I went back to my bed. It was, after all, routine. I couldn't deal with food. I forgot how. When I was in the kitchen, I would go back to my bed, very confused. I had been gone so long that I had no familiarity with the things of everyday living. I can't take it, I thought, I can't live like this . . . useless and hopeless. I had no friends, no job, no hobbies, no church. I lost everything, and to bring it back is way too much to believe in. Months passed with little change.

It has been changing ever so slightly. It takes a long time for me to become used to anything outside my bedroom. Everything seems to have a red flag or a caution sign on it. I don't know if this is necessarily a Morgellons thing or a matter of each individual character. I'd have to guess that each person would go through the whole experience differently.

I'm developing strength now and living on my own for the first time in many years. That's my God! I'm alive but rigid. I'm happy but dull. I'm giving my all, but it doesn't pack a punch. Bottom line, coming back is a gift but one that comes in increments. It is a slow, slow process. I'm now at a place that gives me some excitement without fear of change. It's a huge change, a huge process that no one should have to go through alone. I pray for each and everyone of you out there that doesn't believe healing is worth it. It *is* worth it. I am now convinced that the years to come will be the best years of my life. One cannot lose everything and come back taking things for granted. I savor every moment. I'm loving all the surprises life is bringing me. All the newness still creates fear but it's getting exciting as well! So go on and believe! Stay strong, because you are. You will be able to live again. Keep fighting. Keep winning.

Epilogue

I met Bobbi when she was struggling and fighting a disease called Morgellons. No one knew about it or had heard about it. Looking back at when I met Bobbi, I didn't really know what was going on in her life. At first it was confusing and hard to believe. I saw her as isolated and depressed. She sheltered herself from the world. I believe it was because of confusion and shame and tired of not knowing what was going on. No one believed her, not even doctors. Imagine going through this pain and confusion alone.

I have been there time and time again and have seen/witnessed what was coming out of her skin. I saw it and watched it with my own eyes, the pain and fibers that no one would believe or even listen to her cry for help. She would block me out, even me, due to being embarrassed, ashamed, and again confused and depressed—fighting this terrible disease by herself.

Talk about scared and scarred. I look back at Bobbi, seeing her at her worst, fighting this condition that no one knew about. I have ran to her side when she called, to see things she removed from her skin. She proved over and over again to me that there was something wrong. I believed and could see the pain and fibers come out. I asked her how she knew where and what to look for. She said the pain would direct her to the fibers—a burning pain constantly running through her body. She had no control of it. They kept refusing to test the fibers time and time again. All she could do is suffer by herself, ashamed and depressed. I've seen this many times—all the different fibers that came out of my friend—who separated herself from the world. She was sick not knowing what will happen next or what will come out of her, any minute of the day, trying to control her thoughts and feelings. Bobbi lived this way for years thinking this would never end, waking up worried, in pain with one big painful lesion. I stood behind my friend trying to understand and believe what no one else would. No one!!

I was watching Bobbi go through so much pain and confusion losing hope and precious life. She moved away with relatives hoping for the help she so badly needed. She was gone for almost a year. I had no contact with her when she first came back. After staying with her daughter for several months—Wow! No more pain, no more fibers!! Is my friend cured? She's still struggling with depression, scarred mentally and physically. But their was a glow, a sign that she wanted to live . . . little by little. It took a lot of time and courage to go out into the world and live again after being sheltered and living in fear. Everyday is another step for her. Whether its' a crack in the sidewalk or a stormy rainy day, she keeps her head up and gets through it trying new and different things she hasn't thought of in years. Just waking up happier whether its' riding a bike with me, catching a fish, meeting new friends, writing a book, or just wandering around her home thinking of her next journey or experience. She's slowly healing both mentally and physically. Everyday is one step further on her path with God. The path leading her to a long and fulfilling happy life, putting the past where it belongs for sure—behind her. Bobbi Devine is a true survivor! Definitely!

Malisa A. Weldon

CPSIA information can be obtained
at www.ICGtesting.com
Printed in the USA
FFOW03n1321180418
46307497-47835FF